The Structure of College Choice

Robert Zemsky
Penney Oedel

College Entrance Examination Board
New York, 1983

To John Hobstetter,
who made the asking of questions
a special enterprise

Copies of this book may be ordered from: College Board Publications,
Box 886, New York, New York, 10101. The price is $10.25.

Editorial inquiries concerning this book should be directed to: Editorial
Office, The College Board, 888 Seventh Avenue, New York, New York
10106.

Library of Congress Catalog Number: 83-72152

Printed in the United States of America.

9 8 7 6 5 4 3 2 1

Contents

Tables

Figures

Preface

Five years ago higher education was preoccupied with demographics. Stephen Dresch had already frightened everyone who would listen with his projection of 40-percent declines in college enrollments by the close of the 1980s. Wilson College's court-blocked attempt to close its doors in response to declining enrollments seemed to presage a decade of institutional drift and judicial oversight. Everywhere, the search for nontraditional students reflected a growing conviction that classrooms would soon be empty and dormitories vacant unless American colleges and universities attracted new clientele.

In fact, these last five years have turned out differently than expected. What has troubled colleges and universities most has been not enrollments but finances — the prospect of running out of money long before running out of students. Still, that preoccupation with demographics brought a widespread understanding that the demand for higher education can contract as well as expand. Most educational leaders now accept that by the close of the 1980s, there will be a substantial surplus of seats in the classrooms of America's colleges and universities. Many leaders believe that yesterday's doomsayers were not wrong, just premature.

Higher education's early preoccupation with demographics also highlighted how little was known about the process that transforms high school seniors into college freshmen. Five years ago enrollment planning was a nonsubject on most American campuses. That, too, has changed. College presidents at all types of institutions have made major investments in discovering just who is interested in their campuses and why. Indeed, enrollment research has become something of a growth industry as higher education has sought to become the beneficiary of its own capacity for discovering useful knowledge.

The purpose of this volume is to report on the most comprehensive of the enrollment planning projects generated by this new interest in college admissions. The project began simply enough as a set of planning analyses for the University of Pennsylvania. Asked by our president to estimate the university's undergraduate enrollment potential in the 1980s, we soon discovered that it was impossible to answer his question in isolation. He was asking not only, "Who thinks about Penn?" but also, "What other institutions do they think about when they think about us?" In pursuit of these questions, we began working in 1978 with the Market Research Committee of the Consortium on Financing Higher Education (COFHE). The Consortium, a group of thirty selective private institutions, had in its brief history developed a remarkable tradition of sharing data. Members of COFHE had come to know almost as much about one another's applicant pools as they did about their own.

For nearly a year, the Consortium's Market Research Committee provided focus to our efforts. Much of this project's framework—the Market Segment Model and its derivation from admissions officers' folklore—was shaped and then reshaped in our discussions with members of the committee. Ironically, perhaps, the success of those discussions quickly led us outside of the Consortium, for it became increasingly clear that the Consortium's share of the market was almost as limited as that of our own institution. To gain a truly comprehensive view of the collegiate enrollment market, we needed a database that described most institutions and most students.

At this juncture, we asked the College Board if it might provide the database we required. Coincidentally the Board was reviewing its own efforts to help colleges estimate their enrollment potential, efforts which had faltered largely because the smallest demographic unit used in these analyses was the state. In the spring of 1979, the College Board invited us to design what would become its Comprehensive Undergraduate Enrollment Planning Project (CUEPP). The following fall, under the joint auspices of the Pennsylvania Department of Education and the College Board, we began a full-scale test of the Market Segment Model in the Commonwealth of Pennsylvania.

That pilot study set the tone for the development of the project over the next three years. Superintending our efforts were two remarkable civil servants, Marna Whittington and Philip Mulvihill, and an advisory committee chaired by Fredrick Binder, President of Juniata College. Also serving on the committee were Marvin Wachman, President of Temple University and then chairman of the Pennsylvania Association of Colleges and Universities, and his successor to the chairmanship, Charles Rollins, President of Bucks County Community College. In February 1981, we presented our analysis of the Pennsylvania enrollment market to a special meeting of college presidents and chief academic officers; subsequently we conducted a series of workshops for admissions officers both in Philadelphia and in the western part of the state.

The same pattern was followed in New England, with funds supplied by the College Board and the Ford Foundation and with the co-sponsorship of the New England Board of Higher Education. The advisory panel was chaired by Bruce Poulton, then Chancellor of the University of New Hampshire System, and included representation from all sectors of New England higher education. For this phase of the project, we developed a set of user materials that were tested at regional workshops held in the spring and summer of 1982. Admissions officers from more than 90 percent of New England's four-year institutions and 60 percent of its two-year institutions attended these workshops. Based on our experience with these first-time users of the project's planning materials, the *Field Test Guide* was revised and used at a new series of workshops held in conjunction with the College Board's regional meetings in Boston, Pittsburgh, and Birmingham in the winter of 1983.

The research we describe here thus is based both on a statistical analysis of the collegiate options considered by more than one-half million high school seniors in the eastern third of the nation and, just as importantly, on the experience we have gained in presenting the data to college presidents, chief academic officers, and admissions professionals. The organization of this study parallels the presentations of materials in the public meetings and workshops. We begin in Chapter 1 with a conceptual overview of enrollment planning, suggesting a framework for public and institutional policies as well as a vocabulary to describe the actual workings of the higher education market. Chapter 2 describes the evolution of the Market Segment Model—its origins in the language of the admissions professional and its current applications. Chapter 3 addresses two fundamental questions: "How do students in each segment differ?" and "What makes one high school senior range far from home in developing his or her college choices, while another concentrates almost exclusively on institutions close to home?" Chapter 4 poses the same questions from the institutional point of view: "Which colleges compete most often for national students and which, for local?" and "Is there, in fact, a structure to those competitive relationships?" Chapter 5 deals explicitly with the policy dimensions of our study, looking first at how demographics and the state of the economy combine to establish the rate at which high school seniors go on to participate in higher education. Here the central question we ask is, "Will the demographic and economic events of the 1980s greatly change the current structure of college choice?" We conclude by suggesting some public policy initiatives that might ameliorate the most negative aspects of institutional competition.

Philadelphia   Robert Zemsky
April 1983   Penney Oedel

Acknowledgments

As those who have watched the development of the College Board's Comprehensive Undergraduate Enrollment Planning Project know, ours has been a remarkably collective enterprise. Among our many debts, our greatest are to our collaborators Susan Shaman and Michael Tierney. When she joined our staff in 1978, Susan brought with her precisely that experience in admissions research that made thinking about a market model not only possible but genuinely exciting. Our reach again was extended when Michael joined the Institute as Associate Director in 1980. His independent work on college participation rates and his companion study relating student finances to market segments made major contributions to our analysis. Translation of the Market Segment Model into a computerized production system was Mary Ann Berberich's extraordinary contribution to the project. With care and precision, Larry Logue compiled and verified our statistical data, making sure that, in fact, we meant what we said. Mark Silver and his colleagues, Cecile Feldman and Benjamin Seaver, designed and implemented the microcomputer user system that will become an integral part of CUEPP. Leigh Vogel drew most of the "Tinker Toys" and schematics, while Jo Anne Saporito had the singular and often unenviable responsibility of making sure that we produced on time and correctly the myriad CUEPP materials distributed over the eastern third of the United States.

A host of colleagues provided encouragement as well as critical reviews of our conclusions. As members of COFHE's Market Research Committee, Ted Bracken, now of the COFHE Washington office, Pat Waters of Mt. Holyoke, and Don Dickason of Cornell helped shape our initial efforts. Don, who now serves as Dean of Admissions at the Pennsylvania State University, also shared with us detailed data on

Penn State's Commonwealth campuses and helped develop the project's user materials. Kay Hanson, Executive Director of COFHE, served on our New England Advisory Committee and, more importantly, helped design our public presentations. Her colleague, Larry Litten, shared the insights of his own study of college choice and gave us a detailed reading of our manuscript. Jack Maguire of Boston College, Linda Maguire of Simmons College, and Jeannie Dissette of the University of Pennsylvania were willing subjects of our first experiments in having admissions professionals use CUEPP data to map their institutions' admissions markets.

Jim Nelson, then Vice President of the College Board, was responsible for the project's creation. His willingness to gamble on a small research group will be forever appreciated by those of us who benefited from his confidence and counsel. Pat Peters, Cal Crawford, and Ernie Beals of the College Board's New England, Middle States, and Southern regional offices respectively, provided critical connections to individual colleges and universities. Sue Watts of the College Board's national office has been perceptive critic of most of the project's written materials. We owe her a special debt for helping us clarify the concepts of market and market concentration.

Our largest debt is to Darrell Morris, Executive Director of Data and Special Services of the College Board. He has guided, coaxed, reinforced, and ocassionally chastised us over the last four years, making sure that what we did at each juncture was our best. His belief in the Market Segment Model allowed him to bend its applications in a way that provided maximum utility to the colleges and universities he serves on behalf of the College Board.

We owe a special acknowledgment to Virginia Branch, who took the product of our often disorganized writing sessions and helped transform them into a final product.

1

Language, Symbol, and System: A Framework for Enrollment Planning

As planner for the University of Pennsylvania, John Hobstetter brought not only an engineer's sense of system but also an unexpected elegance and precision of language. Within his prose he could capture both the aspirations of the university community he served and the efforts of administrative leaders to achieve those ambitions. In the mid-1970s, Hobstetter assembled a group of scholars who shared his faith in decentralized planning and observed his standards in putting that faith into practice. Most of us were trained as social scientists, a fact that Hobstetter never let us forget, particularly when we submitted some outlandish piece of prose. Too often we did not know precisely what words meant, so we used them at the wrong time and in the wrong way. *Structure* was a favorite term: we were forever talking about the structure of universities, plans, budgets, departments, programs. In our argot, anything worth analyzing had to have a structure.

One day, his patience all but gone, Hobstetter pointed to a Tinker Toy model of a crystal and said, "When things have structures, you can build a model just like that, representing relations among the relevant parts." We did not realize how deeply he had impressed us that day until much later. After examining the first data from our study of college enrollments, we turned to one another and said, "We can build a Tinker Toy." As bewildered colleagues watched, we rummaged through

1

children's toys, searching for circles of wood to represent individual colleges and connecting rods to indicate competitive relationships. The models we built that afternoon were not so precise as Hobstetter's crystal—no social structure could be—but they possessed the same essential quality. Each structure was ordered: there was only one right way to assemble the pieces so that all of the connections could be made. Just looking at a finished model, one began to have an intuitive understanding of how two colleges that literally sat side by side in Philadelphia could compete so infrequently with one another. Eventually, we stopped building Tinker Toy models, having developed a more easily executed diagram system that conveyed the same structural information. Yet we can still look at the data we have assembled for over a hundred separate admissions markets and visualize what Hobstetter's Tinker Toy would look like if, in fact, we chose to build it.

This study owes another, more traditional debt to John Hobstetter. As members of the planning team he assembled, we were charged with estimating the likely scale of each of the university's schools over the balance of the decade. In the course of this research, we made two discoveries that led us deep into the field of enrollment planning. The first was that although the University of Pennsylvania was a privately endowed research institution, its fastest-growing source of revenue was tuition. By the close of the 1970s, tuition income was 50 percent more important to the university than at the beginning of the decade, making the Dean of Undergraduate Admissions responsible for a larger share of the university's income than the Senior Vice President for Development and University Relations. More than at any time in its recent past, the financial future of the university rested on its ability to increase instructional revenues through a combination of tuition increases and gradual enrollment growth.

Our second discovery was simply that there was little understanding of the degree to which the university's enrollments were at risk. At our institution, as on most campuses, a curious division of labor governed enrollment planning. The admissions office was in charge of generating enrollment. Its staff devised recruiting strategies, reviewed public relations techniques, and estimated the rate at which prospective students would apply and accept. Enrollment levels, however, were set by the central administration—the president, the provost, and senior financial officers in close consultation with key committees of the board of trustees. These discussions were dominated by concerns over inflation, which constantly compelled the university to raise additional revenue. Despite their awareness that the nation's pool of college-aged youths was going to shrink, the university's senior officers opted for budgets that assumed that enrollments could continue to expand. Accordingly, the admissions staff concentrated on gauging short-term market trends.

These circumstances were scarcely unique to the University of Pennsylvania. In the late 1970s, institutions of every type were struggling to reconcile short-term financial needs with long-term enrollment prospects. What most institutions discovered was that preservation of both their financial and their educational integrity would require a better understanding of the structure of the college admissions market. Three types of information were necessary. First, American higher education needed an overview of the market composed of young people planning to attend college. How many college-bound 18-year-olds resided in any given region of the country? What were the backgrounds, interests, and achievements of these students, and what kinds of institutions did they find most attractive? Second, individual institutions needed a summary mapping of their own visibility, showing the total volume and geographic distribution of students with a demonstrated interest in attending their campuses. Finally, a realistic assessment of enrollment prospects required data on competitive market share — in simplest terms, a calculation comparing institutional volume to total market volume, conveying market share as a percentage. To be genuinely useful, however, such analyses needed to be taken a step further: what other types of colleges and universities were each institution's prospective applicants considering?

This final question — the structure of institutional competition — eventually led to the Tinker Toy models, but the answers implicit in those models emerged only after a long process of speculation and conceptualization, testing and retesting. Our analytic goals were clear: to provide both a macroview of the nation's collegiate enrollment markets and a microview of the single institution's visibility. The larger challenge, however, lay in shaping a meaningful form and context for that information. What college and university presidents and planners most surely did not need was yet another deluge of unmanageable data.

Language, not numbers, provided the key. Neither the rhetoric of Cassandra prophesying demographic doom nor the technocratese of marketing consultants spoke effectively to educational leaders. Most college presidents, chancellors, and provosts relied on their admissions officers to filter and translate the enrollment information relevant to internal policy and management decisions. It was the substance and style of these dialogues that furnished the framework for our analysis, lending the necessary logic as well as vocabulary for our quantification of the structure of college choice. Admissions folklore about local "pools" underlay our definition of regional enrollment markets, and the recruiter's intuitive understanding of "feeder high schools" led us to segment those markets according to the geographic horizons of the students' choice sets.

To translate this conceptual framework into a working model, we needed a comprehensive data base reflecting the early stages of college choice. Certainly the first, and most limited, indicator of market visibility would be simple name recognition: Do high school students in a particular area know of the college in question? Although obtainable through surveys, such information suggests little about the likelihood of students applying to or enrolling in that institution. At some point, typically during their junior or senior years, students become more purposeful in their opinions about different colleges. Often this increased interest is occasioned by the opportunity to participate in the Admissions Testing Program of the College Board. As part of registration for the Scholastic Aptitude Test (SAT) and Achievement Tests, students indicate a set of institutions to which they want their test scores sent. Subsequently, many students name additional institutions to which their scores are sent. It is this set of up to 30 designated institutions which, for most college-bound high school seniors, represents the outer limit of student choice.

The value of the information generated by this process lies both in its truly comprehensive character — approximately a million high school students participate each year in the College Board's Admission Testing Program (ATP) — and in its rich description of individual students. As part of their ATP participation, about 90 percent of all students who take the SAT fill out the Student Descriptive Questionnaire (SDQ), which requests information on the student's personal background, achievement, and goals. If there were, in fact, a structure to college choice, the College Board's data would provide a remarkable opportunity to measure the cultural as well as socioeconomic underpinnings of that structure.

For our analysis, we sought not a complex mathematical model, but a straightforward classification system that would track the pattern of SAT-score submissions to create a map of student choice. The Market Segment Model that we developed was nothing more than a set of simple rules for disaggregating high school seniors into similar groups. The model worked because students, once so disaggregated, appeared to behave in remarkably consistent ways. Our initial task was to define enrollment markets in a manner consistent with admissions officers' intuitive understanding of student pools. Three stages of disaggregation were involved: regions (New England, Middle States, and South), states, and community-based markets. We next segmented each market by classifying students residing within the market as local, in-state, regional, or national. These segmentation principles obviously assumed a strong geographic basis for student choice, an assumption everywhere confirmed by the recruiting experiences of admissions officers. The first product of our analysis was a series of publicly distributed Market Segment Profiles, one for each market, that reported the number and type of students in each segment. Also displayed were measures of institutional competition for each market, including statistical descriptions of the five institutions that attracted scores from the greatest number of students in each segment. These data furnished the overview against which individual institutions measured their competitive share of each market segment.

Taken together, the Market Segment Profiles and reports to individual institutions provided the policy dimension to our research. Time and again we had heard about the "business" of collegiate competition, and we had watched admissions marketing grow into a flourishing industry, complete with the standard techniques of marketing a product in oversupply. One simple fact, however, confounded this approach to marketing: colleges are not businesses. If enrollment planning proved manageable only in mass-marketing terms, there would be two sets of losers. First would be the institutions themselves; in the process of scrambling from one recruiting strategy to another, colleges and universities inevitably would deplete their discretionary resources and educational energies. The second set of losers would be the students. Some observers had argued that increased competition among colleges would, as a matter of course, benefit educational consumers, as institutions expanded their offerings and reduced their prices in an effort to attract more students. Yet the marketing that accompanied such efforts could threaten the viability of the product itself. Higher education works largely because access to a college or university is interpreted as a right contingent upon the student's ability to perform, and benefit from, college-level work. To the extent that mass marketing lowered the student's expected contribution to the learning process, the college experience would be devalued.

By reporting to all institutions competing within a given market both the overall contours of that market and their individual shares, we sought to lower the competitive edge some institutions might enjoy simply because they decided to invest substantial sums in extensive market surveys. Indeed, from the outset there was a feeling both within the College Board and among our staff that if the project were successful, it could dramatically reduce the amount of scarce resources being spent on expensive market surveys and public relations campaigns. The materials produced by our research would include much of the information typically provided by marketing consultants hired to measure an institution's market potential and redirect its recruiting campaign. By supplying such aids simultaneously to all participating institutions, we could reduce the per-institution cost to a fraction of the private consultant's bill. More important, the data would contain no competitive bias: each institution would have the same chance to judge its visibility and identify recruiting opportunities. No doubt some institutions would prove more adept than others at making use of the data, but every college had the potential to benefit; no institution would need to worry that a rival's ability to buy market information would enable the rival to siphon off that institution's applicant pool.

In time, resulting changes in the protocol of institutional competition could have a telling impact on public policy attitudes and initiatives. From its inception our research has occupied that half-world between collegiate planning and governmental oversight, where the candle burns at both ends. In recent years, most states have expanded their definition of the state educational system to include all degree-granting institutions—private as well as public, research universities as well as community colleges. In a time of mounting economic and demographic pressures, many colleges tend to assume a defensive posture toward the state, viewing policy makers as potential adversaries rather than as disinterested benefactors. The state, in turn, fears that competitive marketing may divert scarce resources away from basic academic needs, jeopardizing equal access to quality education. All too often, enrollment projections are exploited as one more rhetorical weapon either to defend current allocations or to advocate sharper reductions in public support for higher education. Each new projection is accepted or rejected depending on how it fits into the current tactical situation.

The consistent, comprehensive character of the College Board data and Market Segment Model reduces the tendency toward obfuscation by interjecting reliable definitions of market potential and institutional visibility. Ideally this common ground can serve as a point of departure for productive dialogue between public policy makers and educational leaders as well as for joint ventures among competing colleges and universities. In pursuit of these goals, the Ford Foundation has funded a key portion of our research. What they, and we, envision is a new climate of cooperation in which rational enrollment planning might proceed as a partnership between college and state as well as between college and college through the medium of consortia.

While we speak of ideals, the Market Segment Model is concerned with facts; and it is a fact that the number of 18-year-olds in this country will decline over the next two decades. We accept as a given that there will be fewer, as well as smaller, colleges and universities 20 years from now. Other American institutions have experienced periods of contraction, and we see no reason to believe that higher education is either immune to that process or particularly undermined by the prospect of growing smaller. Denying the inevitability, or perhaps even advisability, of purposeful pruning may be good politics in the short run, but over the longer haul the cost to higher education in terms of self-reliance could prove staggering.

It is our hope that the research described here, along with the institutional planning already occasioned by the Market Segment Model, can help manage this transition to fewer and smaller colleges by supplying the tools for rational communication. If we must recognize the unhappy fact of diminishing applicant pools, let us at least conceive the problem in terms that make sense to collegiate officers rather than pronounce, or renounce, judgments of universal doom. Let us, moreover, guard against the error of casting public policy in accordance with unsubstantiated assumptions about the future of higher education. Several predictions, in particular, have gained currency in the debate over the allocation of public monies to colleges and their students: higher education's future will depend on its ability to reach new markets and nontraditional clientele; the decline in the number of students of traditional age will prove most debilitating to small institutions; escalating tuition costs will force a migration of students, particularly the high-ability group, from the private to the public sector, sparking a public versus private "shoot-out."

Since we know how our story turns out, let us state at the outset that none of these propositions accurately describes the patterns we have observed in our analysis of college choice. To begin, we see no signs that the majority of colleges and universities should abandon their orientation toward traditional-age college students. Most, in fact, will succeed by doing in the future what they have done best in the past. In higher education's highly ordered market, it is difficult for institutions to change their public image. Only a few are likely to save themselves by taking a faculty and physical plant developed for one purpose and converting it to another. Thus, the critical question for almost every institution will be, "How many traditional, full-time students can we count on in the 1980s?" Even community colleges, which often draw less than half their students from this traditional market, will need to know how many of their younger students are likely to seek other options in the more competitive market of the 1980s.

Small colleges, particularly nonselective private institutions, do appear especially vulnerable to declines in the pool of traditional-age students. There will surely be a number of institutional closings over the coming decade, including a few colleges with awkward, mid-range enrollments of 2,500 to 6,000; such institutions could find themselves hard pressed to sustain their fixed costs, given their poor share of the traditional-age student market. We should not, however, understate the diversity of the nation's small colleges. Our data suggest that most of these institutions will prosper despite adverse demographic trends.

Finally, we remain skeptical of any scenario that assumes a rapid migration of students from one sector of the higher education system to another. The patterns of college choice are so closely associated with the key variables of social and familial life in America that it is hard to imagine any short-term economic shock—even the elimination of the Guaranteed Student Loan—suddenly undermining the system of values that currently helps young people and their families decide which colleges and universities to consider for the baccalaureate degree. We simply do not believe there will be a public versus private "shoot-out." For the most part, public institutions compete with public institutions, private institutions with private institutions, small Catholic colleges with other small Catholic colleges, highly selective institutions with other highly selective institutions, and community colleges with other low-cost, locally supported, two-year educational programs. Indeed, what we see in the findings we are about to describe are not so much the seeds of confrontation as the opportunity for cooperation.

To foster both institutional independence and interdependence, to refine both the vocabulary and the information upon which public policy is based—these are, perhaps, grand goals for a study that began with Tinker Toys. For some people, the very simplicity of the Market Segment Model proves oddly disappointing. In its broadest outlines, our research does suggest that college choice is a function of basic social patterning, a finding that should astound no one. Yet as anyone who closely follows admissions marketing knows, the reputations, and hence fortunes, of individual colleges and universities can change: some institutions will gain, others will lose. Our argument, put simply, is that the educational process will be better served if colleges and universities understand to which kind of students they are most visible. Higher education needs less "tilting against windmills" and a more purposeful sense of resolve and cooperation.

2

Knowing the Territory: An Introduction to the Market Segment Model

Admissions officers invariably are tellers of stories — about the colleges they represent, about the colleges they attended, about each other, and about the often vagabond life of college recruiting. Filled with lively humor and good-natured exaggeration, the stories nonetheless have a serious purpose. College recruiting is an intensively competitive calling, yet most of what a good admissions officer knows has been learned from other admissions officers, at conferences or college fair nights, in airports or hotel lobbies. Here the real information of the craft is exchanged: which high schools are changing, where new admissions counselors are making their presence felt, how changes in a state's student assistance program may affect out-of-state recruiters, where there is weakness in a competitor's applicant pool, and which colleges are depending on enrollment growth to balance their budgets.

It is a network that remains largely unappreciated outside its own circle. Indeed, the admissions officers' penchant for anecdotes has led more than one college president to bemoan the lack of analytic conciseness in the very people on whom their institutions have come so heavily to depend. It is a silly mistake. There is little that is happenstance about the admissions officers' understanding. They know full well that high school juniors and seniors, whatever their personal unpredictability, collectively behave in a most predictable fashion when it comes time to select a college. The way to understand that behavior is

9

to get out on the hustings, to serve one's apprenticeship as a school visitor, to run a booth at a college fair. Every chance meeting with colleagues along the road becomes a new occasion to share information, exchange intelligence, and contribute yet another round of stories.

We have begun with this celebration of storytelling for two reasons. First, we believe that the intuitions of admissions officers actually comprise a remarkably systematic body of knowledge about the college selection process. Second, much of that knowledge has been captured in the admissions officers' tales, which exhibit all the hallmarks of a classic folklore: language, symbol, and system. Our research thus is based on listening carefully to what admissions officers have to say.

The college recruiter's basic frame of reference is the community, viewed as an admissions pool or market composed of college-bound high school juniors and seniors. When asked how to define such a market, one admissions officer replied, "It is anywhere within a three-hour radius from a major airport in a rented car." Representing an institution that recruited nationally, this admissions officer had a map emblazoned with a string of such circles—from Chicago, St. Louis, and Atlanta; to Tampa, St. Petersburg, and Miami; and back up along the Atlantic coast to the fertile suburbs of Washington, D.C. Most admissions officers carry such maps in their heads. Institutions that recruit locally simply make finer gradations—the South Shore out of Boston, the 128 suburbs, the North Shore, and the ring of communities beyond Route 425. Meredith Willson's salesman in *The Music Man* made the point best when he observed, "You've got to know the territory."

Yet it would be fundamentally wrong to equate admissions officers with salesmen and to mistake college recruiting for selling. The more apt analogy derives from taking seriously the contention of colleges that they are, in fact, communities. Then college recruiting becomes much like political canvassing. Knowing the territory means understanding both the geographic boundaries of a community and the different kinds of people who live there. The task of the political canvasser is to understand to whom a candidate can most naturally appeal. Who is likely to understand the party represented, the goals of its platforms, and the ideals of its candidates? Political canvassing does not mean converting those who are opposed or indifferent to you; it means making more active those who already are attracted to your banner.[1]

In college recruitment, knowing the territory means understanding which students within which communities are most likely to be attracted to your college. Who knows your institution is out there? Who is prepared to imagine herself or himself as a member of your educational community? As in politics, this sense of potential affiliation seems to be deeply rooted in family values and social tradition. To a surprising degree, the configuration of these factors is consistently reflected in the geographic range of institutions in which a student expresses interest. In the words of one admissions officer, "There are only three kinds of college-bound students: those who want to live at home, those who want to live on campus but bring their laundry home, and those who want to go far enough from home that Mom and Dad can't visit without calling first."

After years of experience, a good admissions professional intuitively understands how to recognize these different types of students and understands how their personal abilities and social backgrounds are expressed through the geographic limits of their collegiate aspirations. A good recruiter also knows where to look for prospective applicants, as seen in the students' willingness or reluctance to travel. It is necessary to identify not only the most promising communities or pools, but also the specific neighborhoods within those communities — hence the recruiter's emphasis on feeder high schools.

From the beginning, we have sought to mold our research to these concepts, to capture and quantify the phenomenon behind the folklore. Thus, it is the admissions officers' notion of admissions pools that dictates the geographic units of our analysis. In dividing up the East Coast, we relied on three types of boundaries — region, state, and community. The three broad regions are those traditionally specified by the College Board: New England (Maine, New Hampshire, Vermont, Massachusetts, Connecticut, Rhode Island), Middle States (New York, New Jersey, Pennsylvania, Delaware, Maryland, Washington, D.C.), and South (Virginia, North Carolina, South Carolina, Georgia, and Florida).

For the purpose of illustration, this study concentrates on the New England region.[2] In part, this decision reflects the fact that it was in New England that we came first to understand the community-based nature of the college admissions market. It is also true, however, that New England has played a critical role in the history of higher education, often serving as a model for the development of colleges and universities throughout the eastern third of the nation. We have made certain, finally, that the key trends we isolate in New England are in fact broadly characteristic of the structure of college choice. Appendix A presents data for the Middle States and South confirming this finding.

Treating each region separately, we divided each state into as few as two and as many as thirty community-based enrollment markets or pools, for a total of 143 separate markets. In many cases, the market boundaries match formal political and educational divisions, reflecting natural channels of communication. Each major metropolitan area is composed of several markets, usually corresponding to the inner city, a first ring of suburbs, and an outer ring of suburbs. In more sparsely populated areas, communities are sometimes combined in order to make the analysis meaningful.[3]

In accordance with the admissions officers' understanding of geographic aspirations, we segmented each market by classifying college-bound high school seniors residing within that market as local, in-state, regional, or national. Local students concentrate on institutions located within their own market. Such students tend to be commuters, are more likely to consider part-time courses of study, and frequently will make the local community college their institution of first choice. In-state students concentrate on colleges and universities within their home state, including local institutions. They are likely to prefer living on campus, and they tend to develop both public and private options. Regional students focus largely on institutions within their own region (New England, Middle States, or South). Interested primarily in institutions located outside their home states, these students, on the average, develop more private than public alternatives. They also include within their options a few key in-state institutions, such as the flagship campus of the state university system. National students concentrate their college interests outside the region. These are the students with the widest geographic aspirations. Though they, too, will develop some regional options, such as the flagship campus of the state university system, this is the segment of the market most committed to private institutions and most willing to bear substantial tuition and living costs in pursuit of educational goals.

Within this framework, the College Board data and the Market Segment Model that contains those data are easily understood. By tracing students' SAT-score submissions, the model simply classifies students according to the geographic range of the institutions in which they express interest. To determine whether a student is local, in-state, regional, or national, we note the location of institutions to which she or he submits test scores: how many are located within the student's own enrollment market, how many within the student's home state, how many within the larger region, how many outside that region. Once each of the designated institutions is thus classified, we ask which of the four categories is largest. In the case of a tie, we accord the student the farthest aspiration. Thus, a student who designates one local, one regional, two in-state, and two national institutions is classified as a national student. Conversely, a student who designates three local, two in-state, one regional, and one national institution is classified as a local student.[4]

To understand what these data tell us about student behavior and institutional visibility, we must first understand the calendar of college choice, which begins for some students as early as the ninth grade, when they select their academic curriculum. For most students, this calendar becomes regularized in the eleventh and twelfth grades when they participate in the College Board's Admissions Testing Program, taking first the PSATS and then the SATS and Achievement Tests. The vast majority of SAT-taking students also fill out the Student Descriptive Questionnaire, which requests such information as class rank, academic goals, curricular preference, family income level, and parental education. Students who so elect may have their names, addresses, and basic characteristics included in the College Board's Student Search Service, which allows institutions to purchase mailing lists of students who fit selected criteria. Thus, in their junior year, most high school students who participate in the Admissions Testing Program begin receiving a variety of materials from colleges and universities.

At the same time, these students take an important step in identifying the set of institutions in which they have an interest. Each time a student registers for an examination, he or she is asked to designate institutions to receive the scores. Three such test-score submissions are included in the cost of the examination itself; thereafter, each additional submission carries a modest fee. It is at this point (for some students in their junior year, for most others in the fall of their senior year), that the process of college choice is most in the student's hands. In asking that her or his scores be sent to a particular institution, the student is saying, "I know you're there, here I am." The student may already have applied to the institution, may have written for an application, or may simply intend to write for such an application. One thing, however, is certain: at that moment, a particular set of institutions can be said to be visible to the student.

The distinction between visibility and application or enrollment is an important one, which raises two caveats in interpretation of the market segment data. First, there obviously can be no direct translation of test-score submissions to applications; most institutions receive many more scores than applications. However, as a gauge of potential application, the data allow an institution to focus precisely on the issue of conversion—how to convert interest into choice.[5] Second, in some cases the data on SAT-score submissions actually will understate collegiate visibility, especially for institutions that draw most of their students from the immediate vicinity. Sometimes, SAT scores are conveyed via transcripts; other times, an institution (particularly one that seeks new clientele) will waive the requirement for SATS; and some institutions, such as community colleges, simply do not require the examination. Students, however, often will send scores even to institutions that do not require the SAT, for the perceived link between SAT-score submission and college choice is pervasive.

These definitions of institutional visibility and market segmentation are based on the insights and experiences of admissions professionals. Their folklore has taught us not only what to measure but how to measure it. In the process, we have learned a further lesson in communication. The analytic premise of our research grew out of listening to the way people talked; to bring that understanding full circle, our findings should speak in an equally direct voice. Two levels of information are generated by the Market Segment Model: a macroview, describing all the SAT-taking students and all the competing institutions within a given market; and a microview, detailing the single institution's draw and standing within that market. Through the Market Segment Profile and the Institutional Profile, we have sought to convey both levels of information in a concise, accessible format.

The Market Segment Profile is each market's signature, a detailing of student choice and institutional standing within each segment of that market. In a single-page format, this information is presented for each of the 143 markets currently included in the Comprehensive Undergraduate Enrollment Planning Project. Figure 2.1 illustrates the Market Segment Profile for Fairfield County, Connecticut. The four column headings denote the market segments—local, in-state, regional, and national. Horizontally, the display is divided into an upper and a lower grid. The upper grid provides measures of institutional visibility; the lower grid describes the characteristics of test takers in each of the four segments of the Fairfield County market.

In the first cell of the lower grid, we find a description of students in the local segment of this market—that is, high school seniors residing in Fairfield County who sent most of their SAT scores to colleges and universities located in Fairfield County. In 1980 there were 550 such students, or just under 8 percent of all Fairfield County students who submitted scores. Their average SAT score, verbal and mathematical combined, was 770. The next measure reports the average number of score submissions per test taker. The College Board allows three such submissions without requiring an additional fee; thus, the number of institutions to which a student sends test scores suggests the level of his or her market activity. On the average, students in the local segment of the Fairfield County market sent test scores to only 2.8 institutions.

The remaining information in the lower grid is labeled "Self-Reported" because it is drawn from the Student Descriptive Questionnaire, which is filled out by just under 90 percent of all SAT-taking stu-

Figure 2.1. Sample Market Segment Profile
Connecticut Market 3: Fairfield County

Test Score Submissions

	Local			In-State			Regional			National		
	No.	%	Type	No.	%	Type	No.	%	Type	No.	%	Type
1.	277	50.4	3	757	63.1	2*	610	36.7	2*	1226	32.6	2*
2.	261	47.5	3	515	43.0	3*	348	20.9	2	371	9.9	2
3.	183	33.3	3	438	36.5	3*	272	16.3	2	327	8.7	1
4.	103	18.7	2*	183	15.3	3*	248	14.9	2*	312	8.3	2
5.	100	18.2	3*	177	14.8	3*	197	11.8	2*	308	8.2	2

	Local	In-State	Regional	National
No. of institutions at 5 percent:	11	12	24	17
Percent of all scores going to 5 percent institutions:	84.3	69.6	51.2	26.8

Student Descriptors

	Local	In-State	Regional	National
Total test takers:	550	1,199	1,664	3,766
Average SAT (V + M):	770	850	970	980
Average # scores per test taker:	2.8	3.5	4.8	5.3
Self-Reported				
Percent in top quintile:	27.8	26.1	44.7	45.7
% aspiring to more than B.A.:	30.6	41.5	54.5	62.2
% family income more than $35,000:	11.2	20.6	41.9	43.0
% both parents with B.A.:	9.0	16.3	34.0	37.1

Legend for Institutional Type

* = public
1 = major research university
2 = doctoral-granting university
3 = comprehensive college
4 = liberal arts college
5 = two-year institution
6 = other

dents. On any given question, slightly over 80 percent will provide an answer. The questionnaire thus allows us to describe about 70 percent of the test-taking population in terms of a critical set of personal and familial characteristics. The first of these measures, "Percent in top quintile," specifies the percentage of students in the local segment who reported that they were in the top 20 percent of their high school class. On the average, about 41 percent of all participating Fairfield County students (local, in-state, regional, and national combined) reported themselves in the top 20 percent of the class. For the local market segment, however, this percentage was considerably lower; only 27.8 percent of the students reported that their grades placed them in the upper fifth of their class.

The three remaining measures have played a signal role in our analysis of student choice. The first, percentage of students aspiring to more than a baccalaureate, shows the extent to which students believe that the undergraduate degree is a transitional, rather than a final, step in their education. For the local segment in Fairfield County, only about 31 percent of the students reported that they intended to seek a higher degree. The next item, percentage of students reporting annual family income in excess of $35,000, is the basic economic measure used in our analysis. Viewed more as a ranking of students than a discrete measure of actual family income, the $35,000 figure corresponds roughly to the family income necessary for educational options that require a substantial parental contribution. Approximately 11 percent of the Fairfield County students classified as local reported family income in this range. Finally, test takers report on the educational levels of their parents. For the local market segment in Fairfield County, 9 percent of the participating students reported that both their parents had earned the baccalaureate degree.

The three other cells in the lower grid of the Market Segment Profile contain, in a format identical to the one just examined, information about the other three segments of the student population in Fairfield County—those who sent most of their scores to institutions located in Connecticut (but outside of Fairfield County), those who sent most of their scores to out-of-state New England institutions, and those who sent most of their scores to institutions outside of New England. When we compare the data across segments, a startling pattern emerges. With the exception of a single entry (the percentage of in-state students reporting their class rank in the upper quintile) all the numbers increase from left to right. Average SAT scores and average number of scores per test taker increase consistently from local to national. Among the three critical personal and familial measures, that pattern is repeated. The percentage of students aspiring to more than a baccalaureate ranges from a low of 30.6 percent for local students to a high of 62.2 percent for national students. The proportion of Fairfield County students reporting family income in excess of $35,000 ranges from a low of 11.2 percent in the local segment to a high of 43.0 percent in the national segment. Finally, the educational level of the students' families follows the same pattern: 9 percent of the local students reported that both parents had earned the baccalaureate, while 37.1 percent of the national students reported this to be the case.

It is also revealing to split the lower grid in half, mentally linking local with in-state and regional with national. When we combine the two latter categories, we discover the extent to which Fairfield County, a highly suburban and cosmopolitan community, is an "export market." In fact, the number of students whose aspirations lead them to look beyond the state's border exceeds the number who confine their choices to Connecticut by 3,681. Still splitting the grid in half, we find that the gap between in-state and regional statistics tends to be greater than the difference between local and in-state or regional and national. For example, the number of students with self-reported family income above $35,000 jumps by 21 percentage points between in-state and regional, as compared to 9 points between local and in-state and only 1 point between regional and national.

Clearly what the Market Segment Model has captured is a social and familial dimension to college choice, no surprise to anyone familiar with the literature or friendly with admissions recruiters. In our sample market, students who concentrated their interest outside the New England region scored higher on the SAT, submitted their scores to more institutions, ranked higher in self-reported academic achievement and aspiration, and reported higher parental income and education than their counterparts in the regional, in-state, and local segments. The same general pattern occurs in a comparison of regional with in-state and local students and in a comparison of the in-state and local segments. As we shall see, this left-to-right ordering is not unique to Fairfield County or to other, similarly cosmopolitan markets; rather, the pattern reflects the inherently predictable structure of college choice.

The upper grid of the Market Segment Profile reports measures of institutional competition and market concentration for each of the four student-defined market segments. In the first cell, which again corresponds to the local segment, the upper grid provides a statistical description of the five institutions that attracted scores from the greatest number of students in the local segment of Fairfield County. The first column gives the number of students who sent scores to each of these five institutions. The second column expresses this number as a percentage of total test takers in the local segment. A third column, labeled "Type," identifies each of the top five institutions according to the Carnegie Commission's 1973 institutional classification system. Thus, the top-ranking institution for the local segment receives scores from 277 students, or 50.4 percent of the 550 test takers classified as local. This institution is a "type 3," a comprehensive college. The absence of an asterisk indicates that it is a private institution.

By reading across the upper grid, we can compare and contrast features of institutional competition among the four segments. Note, for example, the extent to which the in-state competition is public: all five top-ranked institutions in this segment—a doctoral-granting university and four comprehensive colleges—are public institutions. The national segment, by contrast, shows only one public institution among the top five, again a doctoral-granting university. Note, too, the relative dominance of the top-ranked institution in each of the segments. In the national segment, the percentage column shows a sharp drop from 32.6 to 9.9 for the first-ranked and second-ranked institutions, indicating the overriding influence of the top institution, a situation that does not apply in the other segments.

The two remaining items of data in the cells of the upper grid constitute measures of market concentration. Looking again at the local cell, the first measure of market concentration cites the number of institutions receiving scores from 5 percent or more of the test takers in the segment. It is a generalized measure of persistent market visibility. The second measure shows what percentage of all local scores was received by this group of institutions—that is, the proportion of market activity accounted for by these persistently visible institutions. Two general rules of thumb govern our definition of market concentration. In a highly concentrated market segment, (1) fewer than fifteen institutions are persistently visible, and (2) these institutions collectively account for at least 60 percent of the student activity in that segment. In Fairfield County, the local and in-state segments are highly concentrated, while the regional and national segments are not. Indeed, in these latter segments neither of the two conditions is met.

Again, the patterns we observe in Fairfield County are typical of many eastern markets. In local and in-state segments, institutions that compete successfully are, with few exceptions, highly visible. In regional and national segments, the competition is more open, as a larger number of institutions achieve persistent visibility without coming to dominate the market. Interpreted jointly with the information in the lower grid of the Market Segment Profile, these data reinforce our impression of linkage among several types of variables—socioeconomic characteristics, geographic aspirations, and competitive structure. As we shall see, institutional competition within local segments is the most intense as well as the most concentrated, focusing on students with few social and familial resources. In-state students are only slightly less likely to concentrate their collegiate options among a relatively few institutions. They bring with them greater social and familial resources and by and large have a determined bias in favor of public as opposed to private institutions. Finally, regional and national students, rich in terms of family income and parental education, develop a greater number of collegiate alternatives. In the New England and Middle States regions, regional and national students concentrate on private options. In the South, however, public institutions play a major role in all four segments. The strength of such institutions in this region offers a persuasive incentive for southern students who might otherwise be classified as national to concentrate their options among institutions in the South.

The Institutional Profile is a confidential report rather than a public one; every college and university receives data showing its share of each market segment from which it receives ten or more scores. The totals for each segment and for the four segments combined are further disaggregated according to nine curricular categories reflecting the students' first choices of curriculum as self-reported in the Student Descriptive Questionnaire. The information for each state is divided into two parts: a state total report and individual reports for all the markets within the state. In the following discussion, we will examine sample data for a private liberal arts college with a wide geographic base and a variety of curricular offerings.

Begin by studying the state total report for Connecticut (Figure 2.2), our sample institution's home state. All the numbers in this display are arrayed under five column headings corresponding to the four market segments plus a total. The box at the top of the report summarizes the sample institution's market share in Connecticut, listing the number of scores received from each market segment and expressing that share as a percentage of all test takers in the segment. The third column, for example, indicates that 343 of the Connecticut students classified as regional—that is, who submitted most of their scores to out-of-state New England institutions—sent scores to our sample institution. In all, there were 7,170 students classified as regional in Connecticut; thus, the sample institution's share of the regional market in Connecticut is 343/7,170, or 4.8 percent. The remaining data in this column disaggregate these figures by curricular preference. Of the 343 regional students who sent scores to our sample institution, 196 expressed a prefer-

Figure 2.2. Sample Institutional Profile

Connecticut Market: State Total

Institutional Profile: Sample Institution
Connecticut Market: State Total

	Students				
	Local	*In-State*	*Regional*	*National*	*Total*
Total Number of Scores Received	55	258	343	394	1,050
Percent of All Test Takers	2.1	5.1	4.8	3.8	4.2

Curriculum Choice	*Local*	*In-State*	*Regional*	*National*	*Total*
Liberal Arts					
Inst. Share	21	121	196	186	524
% Share	3.4	9.3	9.2	6.0	7.3
Engineering					
Inst. Share	2	9	17	21	49
% Share	1.1	2.8	3.8	2.2	2.6
Fine Arts					
Inst. Share	9	27	23	36	95
% Share	4.1	6.2	3.9	3.0	3.9
Applied Health					
Inst. Share	1	6	5	4	16
% Share	0.3	1.1	1.1	1.2	1.0
Education					
Inst. Share	3	5	6	3	17
% Share	1.9	1.2	1.7	0.9	1.3
Business					
Inst. Share	7	26	14	20	67
% Share	1.4	3.2	1.2	1.7	1.8
Applied Land Science					
Inst. Share	3	3	1	2	9
% Share	11.1	3.6	0.5	0.8	1.6
Other					
Inst. Share	9	47	66	100	222
% Share	1.5	5.3	4.3	3.8	3.9
Undecided					
Inst. Share	0	14	15	22	51
% Share	0.0	6.2	5.8	6.3	5.5

ence for the liberal arts. These 196 students constituted 9.2 percent of all regional students interested in the liberal arts.

The data that follow the state total report in the Institutional Profile disaggregate these figures for each of the Connecticut markets from which the institution received ten or more scores. The format for the individual market reports is identical to that of the state total display. In the Fairfield County market (Figure 2.3), for example, a total of 237 students, or 3.3 percent of all test takers in Fairfield County, submitted scores to our sample institution.

What do the state total data reveal about the sample institution's market share? Start with the totals in the summary box. In Massachusetts, our sample institution attracted scores from 1,006 students, or 2.1 percent of the total test takers in the state (Figure 2.4). This figure would seem to suggest low visibility or market share; as a convenient benchmark, 5 percent generally indicates strong visibility for a large institution; 1 percent, for a very small institution. Look next at the summary data for each of the four segments. Only ten local students, 0.1 percent of the total test takers in the local segment of Massachusetts, submitted scores to our sample institution. While 127 in-state students sent scores, this figure still represents only 0.5 percent of the segment. Neither of these results is surprising, given our sample institution's location in Connecticut. In the regional segment, however, 490 students sent scores—a figure well above the 5-percent visibility benchmark. While less dramatic, the activity in the national segment is still promising, with a 3.7-percent share.

The analysis of this institution's target population can be narrowed even further by studying the curricular array to determine the academic interests of interested students. Check first to see whether or not the public perception of the institution's programs matches the available curricula. For example, the Massachusetts state total for our sample institution (Figure 2.4) shows two regional students whose first choice is applied land science, even though this institution does not offer that curriculum. Our sample institution is geared primarily toward students who seek a liberal arts curriculum. The state total data in the Institutional Profile for Massachusetts show how many of the students sending scores to the sample institution expressed a preference for the liberal arts. The total column reports that 477, or 3.3 percent of all Massachusetts test takers with an interest in the liberal arts, sent scores to the sample institution. When we focus, however, on regional and national students—our targeted segments—the market shares jump to 9.6 and 5.0 percent respectively, indicating excellent visibility.

Figure 2.3. Sample Institutional Profile

Connecticut Market 3: Fairfield County

Institutional Profile: Sample Institution
Connecticut Market 3: Fairfield County

	Students				
	Local	*In-State*	*Regional*	*National*	*Total*
Total Number of Scores Received	1	58	69	109	237
Percent of All Test Takers	0.2	4.8	4.1	2.9	3.3
Curriculum Choice	*Local*	*In-State*	*Regional*	*National*	*Total*
Liberal Arts					
Inst. Share	0	25	35	61	121
% Share	0.0	8.4	7.0	5.3	5.9
Engineering					
Inst. Share	0	2	5	3	10
% Share	0.0	3.0	5.8	0.8	1.8
Fine Arts					
Inst. Share	1	9	9	10	29
% Share	2.2	7.3	5.5	2.0	3.4
Applied Health					
Inst. Share	0	3	2	1	6
% Share	0.0	4.1	2.8	0.9	1.8
Education					
Inst. Share	0	1	1	0	2
% Share	0.0	1.0	1.1	0.0	0.6
Business					
Inst. Share	0	5	1	6	12
% Share	0.0	2.3	0.3	1.2	1.0
Applied Land Science					
Inst. Share	0	2	0	0	2
% Share	0.0	8.0	0.0	0.0	1.4
Other					
Inst. Share	0	7	12	20	39
% Share	0.0	3.0	3.6	2.6	2.6
Undecided					
Inst. Share	0	4	4	8	16
% Share	0.0	6.2	6.8	5.6	5.8

Figure 2.4. Sample Institutional Profile

Massachusetts Market: State Total

Institutional Profile: Sample Institution
Massachusetts Market: State Total

	Students				
	Local	*In-State*	*Regional*	*National*	*Total*
Total Number of Scores Received	10	127	490	379	1,006
Percent of All Test Takers	0.1	0.5	6.5	3.7	2.1

Curriculum Choice	*Local*	*In-State*	*Regional*	*National*	*Total*
Liberal Arts					
Inst. Share	8	77	235	157	477
% Share	0.4	1.1	9.6	5.0	3.3
Engineering					
Inst. Share	0	5	7	8	20
% Share	0.0	0.2	1.7	0.7	0.5
Fine Arts					
Inst. Share	0	14	38	31	83
% Share	0.0	0.6	7.6	2.4	1.8
Applied Health					
Inst. Share	0	1	4	1	6
% Share	0.0	0.0	0.9	0.4	0.2
Education					
Inst. Share	0	1	3	1	5
% Share	0.0	0.1	0.8	0.3	0.2
Business					
Inst. Share	1	5	23	18	47
% Share	0.1	0.1	2.2	2.0	0.7
Applied Land Science					
Inst. Share	0	0	2	0	2
% Share	0.0	0.0	0.7	0.0	0.2
Other					
Inst. Share	1	18	145	139	303
% Share	0.1	0.5	8.9	5.2	3.3
Undecided					
Inst. Share	0	6	33	24	63
% Share	0.0	0.6	8.6	6.0	3.0

Figure 2.5. Sample Institutional Profile

Massachusetts Market 3: Fitchburg-North Worchester County

Institutional Profile: Sample Institution
Massachusetts Market 3: Fitchburg–North Worcester County

	Students				
	Local	*In-State*	*Regional*	*National*	*Total*
Total Number of Scores Received	0	3	10	10	23
Percent of All Test Takers	0.0	0.2	3.6	2.3	1.1

Curriculum Choice	*Local*	*In-State*	*Regional*	*National*	*Total*
Liberal Arts					
Inst. Share	0	1	3	2	6
% Share	0.0	0.3	3.3	1.6	1.0
Engineering					
Inst. Share	0	0	1	0	1
% Share	0.0	0.0	4.5	0.0	0.5
Fine Arts					
Inst. Share	0	0	1	0	1
% Share	0.0	0.0	5.9	0.0	0.5
Applied Health					
Inst. Share	0	0	0	0	0
% Share	0.0	0.0	0.0	0.0	0.0
Education					
Inst. Share	0	0	0	0	0
% Share	0.0	0.0	0.0	0.0	0.0
Business					
Inst. Share	0	0	0	0	0
% Share	0.0	0.0	0.0	0.0	0.0
Applied Land Science					
Inst. Share	0	0	0	0	0
% Share	0.0	0.0	0.0	0.0	0.0
Other					
Inst. Share	0	0	5	8	13
% Share	0.0	0.0	9.4	6.7	3.5
Undecided					
Inst. Share	0	2	0	0	2
% Share	0.0	5.7	0.0	0.0	3.2

In this way, moving from a consideration of overall market share (2.1 percent) to the share of a particular segment (6.5 percent) to the share of a particular curricular choice within that segment (9.6 percent), our sample institution can conclude that Massachusetts already represents very fertile ground for recruitment. Assured of the institution's strong basic visibility in the state, the admissions staff can now concentrate on conversion, persuading prospective applicants to apply and, if admitted, enroll.

The individual market reports contained in the Institutional Profile can help translate the general insights of the state total analysis into more specific recruiting plans. The individual market data should be read in the same way as the state total data, beginning with the total columns for scores received and percentage of test takers. Then identify the most promising segments and review the curricular choice array, checking for accuracy of student perception as well as percentage share of key categories. When focusing on a key curricular category, check for strengths and weaknesses across the different markets within a single state. In Market 3 of Massachusetts, the rural Fitchburg and North Worcester County area (Figure 2.5), our sample institution drew only 3.3 percent of the regional segment and 1.6 percent of the national segment in the liberal arts category. This market shows as a "hole" when we contrast its shares to the state total percentages of 9.6 and 5.0 respectively (see Figure 2.4). The contrast is even more striking when we turn to Market 10, the Malden-Lexington-Waltham area (Figure 2.6), where the percentages for the liberal arts category are 18.7 for regional and 7.4 for national. Clearly, our sample institution can build on its strengths in the more prosperous suburban regions; long-range targets might include areas that show signs of converting from a rural to a suburban economy.

In this way, the Institutional Profile and the Market Segment Profile quantify the admission officers' intuitive grasp of market structure. Structure here carries a dual meaning, connoting both the structure of student choice and the structure of institutional competition—the forces shaping college-bound students' decisions and the institutional consequences of those decisions. This two-sided interpretation furnishes the essential framework for planning by individual colleges and universities as well as by public policy makers. To draw effectively on its own natural constituency, a college not only must contact the "right" kind of students—that is, students who are predisposed toward that type of institution—but also must persuade them of its special character. This means knowing the competition as well as the clientele. For

Figure 2.6. Sample Institutional Profile

Massachusetts Market 10: Malden-Lexington-Waltham

Institutional Profile: Sample Institution
Massachusetts Market 10: Malden-Lexington-Waltham

		Students		
	Local	*In-State*	*Regional*	*National*	*Total*
Total Number of Scores Received	0	19	86	78	183
Percent of All Test Takers	0.0	0.8	13.1	6.8	4.2

Curriculum Choice	*Local*	*In-State*	*Regional*	*National*	*Total*
Liberal Arts					
Inst. Share	0	14	42	28	84
% Share	0.0	1.9	18.7	7.4	6.3
Engineering					
Inst. Share	0	0	0	1	1
% Share	0.0	0.0	0.0	1.0	0.3
Fine Arts					
Inst. Share	0	2	3	7	12
% Share	0.0	1.0	8.8	6.0	3.4
Applied Health					
Inst. Share	0	0	1	0	1
% Share	0.0	0.0	3.7	0.0	0.4
Education					
Inst. Share	0	1	0	0	1
% Share	0.0	0.7	0.0	0.0	0.5
Business					
Inst. Share	0	1	2	5	8
% Share	0.0	0.3	2.7	5.9	1.4
Applied Land Science					
Inst. Share	0	0	2	0	2
% Share	0.0	0.0	13.3	0.0	3.6
Other					
Inst. Share	0	1	30	31	62
% Share	0.0	0.2	15.8	8.9	5.9
Undecided					
Inst. Share	0	0	6	6	12
% Share	0.0	0.0	14.0	9.5	5.4

public policy, this dual focus is at once more explicit and more paradoxical. In seeking to understand the needs and interests of different segments of the college-bound population, public policy makers also must respond to the needs of different sectors of the higher education system serving that populace.

These twin dimensions of college choice dictate the form and content of the market segment data. The Institutional Profile records competitive share as well as actual volume at every level of disaggregation, and the Market Segment Profile literally is split in half. As we move now to a more detailed analysis first of student choice and then of institutional competition, these basic reports will remain our road maps, extensions of the stories that tell us about the territory.

Notes

1. Michael Tierney was the first to suggest that admissions recruiting more closely resembles political canvassing than mass marketing.

2. This study is based on test-score submissions from the following sources: Commonwealth of Pennsylvania, 1978–79 test cycle; New England and Pennsylvania, 1979–80 test cycle; New England, Middle States, and South (five specified states only), 1980–81 test cycle. The preliminary analysis was first published in Robert Zemsky, Susan Shaman, Mary Ann Berberich, "Toward an Understanding of College Enrollment: A First Test of the Market Segment Model," *Journal of Education Finance* (1980) 5:355–374. All examples in the ensuing text and figures are drawn from the 1979–80 test cycle for New England.

3. Appendices B1 through B3 list the markets in each of the three regions and illustrate their geographic boundaries. Specific maket data are available in each region's Field Test Guide and Market Segment Profiles published by the Higher Education Finance Research Institute for the College Board (1982). In the case of the South, data were processed for the five states with the highest rates of ATP participation: Florida, Georgia, North Carolina, South Carolina, and Virginia.

4. Technically, the model classifies each student according to the category of institutions to which he or she sends the most scores — local, in-state, regional, or national — ignoring the fact that local is a special subset of in-state and in-state is, in turn, a special subset of regional. In New England, for example, a student who sends scores to two local institutions, two in-state (but not local) institutions, and three out-of-state New England institutions is classified as a regional student, though, in fact, scores were sent to four in-state institutions. Similarly, a student who sends one score to a local institution, one score to an in-state (but not local) institution, one score to an out-of-state New England institution, and two scores to institutions outside of New England will be classified as a national student, though, in fact, scores were sent to three New England institutions. In actual practice very few of these examples occur; most students send most of their scores to institutions in their modal category — local, in-state (but not local), out-of-state New England, or institutions outside of New England. For a discussion of the stability of market segments over time see Appendix C.

5. Using data from the Pennsylvania Higher Education Assistance Agency (PHEAA), Michael Tierney has shown that students are, in fact, likely to matriculate at institutions located within the geographic boundaries described by the students' market segment classifications (see Appendix D).

3

A Sense of Place: Students, Families, and Communities

College choice is often a family affair. Among the more affluent families in which higher education has become a tradition, the selection of a college takes on a ritual air: attendance at school-sponsored meetings, participation in "college nights," travel to distant campuses. Less mobile families rely more on high school counselors and recruiting mail to inform them of the range of college options. In their six-city study, Larry Litten and his colleagues have shown how students and their parents tend to develop parallel, though not identical, preferences. Parents' choices are more likely to reflect the limits of family income and a reluctance to send the student too far from home. The student's preferences are more sensitive to peer opinions and the need to maintain a sense of social belonging. Sometime before graduation, the student's and parents' considerations are molded into a single choice set. Students then have the largest voice in deciding where to enroll.[1]

The Market Segment Model's classification of SAT-score submissions captures this process somewhere near its beginning. The first group of institutions to which a student sends SAT scores probably represents a minimum set of the student's own preferences or at least a set of colleges and universities with which she or he is familiar—because a friend went there, because the family has discussed it, or because the high school counselor has recommended it. The student then begins to convert interest into intention, instructing the College Board to send scores to additional institutions. The college choice set is becoming more purposeful, more reflective of both the students' and the parents' aspirations.

What characterizes these options is their basic consistency, leading us to conclude that students and their families organize the process of college choice by choosing among just a handful of often very similar institutions. The analytic task before us is to explain why some students develop very limited localized options, while others consider a geographically dispersed set of institutions. As we have seen, the Market Segment Profile's left-to-right ordering of data for individual enrollment markets suggests that geographic aspirations are strongly associated with certain social and economic characteristics. On average, do these patterns hold true for each of the three regions — New England, Middle States, and South? What is the degree of variance among individual communities? Is it possible, in other words, to infer market segment from socioeconomic characteristics and vice versa? In the process of answering these questions, we can learn much about the structure of college choice — the role of personal aspirations, family background, and community influence — as well as the underlying logic of effective recruiting strategies.

From the four basic student/family characteristics reported in the Market Segment Profile — student aspirations, family income, parental education, and SAT scores — we have derived four attributes whose presence seems to boost the geographic range of a student's college choice. Again, New England will serve as our example, though the patterns we report are equally characteristic of the Middle States and South (see Appendix A). In 1980 each of approximately 96,500 New England high school seniors sent SAT scores to at least one 2-year or 4-year college or university. For this group, the in-state segment was the largest, with 34,528 students; followed by 26,582 in the national segment; 22,926 regional; and 12,532 local (Table 3.1). Combining local

Table 3.1. Distribution and SATs of New England Students

	Local	In-State	Regional	National
Students	12,532	34,528	22,926	26,582
Percent of Total Classifiable Students				
($N = 96,568$)	13.0	35.8	23.7	27.5
Mean SAT (V + M)	800	870	950	990
Median SAT (V + M)	790	860	940	990
Standard Deviation	180	180	195	210

Table 3.2. Students with Selected Attributes

Attributes	Local	In-State	Regional	National
1. *Degree Aspirations*				
Students responding	11,208	31,387	19,888	21,781
Percent seeking more than a				
baccalaureate	24.6	33.1	42.0	49.7
2. *Parental Education*				
Students responding	10,854	30,658	19,494	21,193
Percent with both parents having				
a baccalaureate	7.5	12.7	24.6	29.6
3. *SAT Scores*				
Students with valid scores	11,921	33,539	22,282	25,748
Percent with combined (V + M)				
score of 1100 or more	5.9	11.8	22.7	31.4
4. *Parental Income*				
Students responding	9,664	26,697	16,460	17,636
Percent with parents earning				
$35,000 or more	5.5	11.1	20.2	24.0

with in-state and regional with national, we find an almost equal division between within-state and out-of-state segments (47,060 versus 49,508). When the four segments are mapped against the following four attributes, some suggestive patterns begin to emerge (Table 3.2).

1. *Students Who Plan to Pursue a Post-Baccalaureate Degree*

More than one-third (32,336 out of 84,264) of the high school seniors answering this question on the Student Descriptive Questionnaire reported that their higher education plans did not terminate with the baccalaureate degree. For these students, college was the next, rather than the final, step in the education process. The kinds of collegiate options these students developed might have reflected a self-positioning for that additional process of examination and application that would come four years hence. Certainly the institutions in which they showed interest were significantly different from those identified by students who did not plan for post-baccalaureate education. In Table 3.2 we find the same persistent left-to-right ordering that we saw in the Market Segment Profile. Thus, local students are much less likely to seek post-baccalaureate education than are national students, with in-state and regional students occupying the intermediate points on the scale. It is important to note, however, that even in the national segment there are more students not planning to seek a post-bacca-laureate degree than planning to do so. Put simply, educational aspiration in and of itself does not allow us to predict a student's market segment.

2. *Students from Families in Which Both Parents Have Earned a Baccalaureate Degree (Student-Reported)*
A similar pattern emerges when we focus on parental education. Just under 16,000 test takers (19.2 percent of the 82,199 students answering this question) reported that both parents had earned the baccalaureate degree. The distribution of these students among the four market segments closely follows the distribution of students from high-income families, and indeed there is a strong correlation between the two. These data allow us to say with considerable confidence that local and in-state students are not likely to come from families in which both parents have received college educations. Just over 70 percent of the students from families in which both parents have college degrees concentrated their college choices among regional and national institutions as opposed to local or in-state institutions. The implication is simply that college-educated parents instill in their children more wide-ranging educational aspirations.

3. *Students with* SAT *Scores (Verbal Plus Math) of 1100 or More*
In Table 3.2 the distribution of students with high SAT scores follows the pattern with which we have now become familiar.[2] Among those who concentrated their college choices locally, less than 6 percent were high-ability students as measured by the SAT. Only 11.8 percent of the in-state segment had SAT scores equal to or in excess of 1100, while 22.7 percent of the regional students and 31.4 percent of the national students scored at or above 1100.

4. *Students from Families with Annual Incomes of at Least $35,000 (Student-Reported)*
Nearly 16 percent of those students responding to the question reported that their families had annual incomes of at least $35,000 per year. That sum is important, for it is near the upper limit of family income qualifying for student financial aid. The students from these families are unlikely to receive grants from state higher education assistance agencies or grants of institutional funds from the colleges they attend. Only a small percentage of all students met or exceeded this income condition; even in the national segment only 24 percent of the students came from high-income families.

Yet the left-to-right ordering of the data does allow us to say that there is little probability that a local student will come from a high-income family. Indeed, we could predict that all local students would come from moderate-income or low-income families and be wrong only 5.5 percent of the time. In-state students were only slightly more likely to come from high-income families — a finding that bears on the role of public institutions in in-state markets. Once we move across the regional barrier, the concentration of higher-income families becomes more pronounced, with nearly one out of every four national students coming from a family with an annual income of $35,000 or more. Just under 70 percent of all students from such families concentrated their collegiate choices among regional and national schools.

The significance of these patterns is at least partially compromised by the unusually high number of students who did not answer the family-income question. On the average, the response rate to questions used in our analysis was slightly less than 86 percent. The response rate for the family-income question, however, was only 73 percent, and the actual number of nonrespondents, 26,111, was nearly twice the average number of nonrespondents on other questions. Common wisdom holds that most of the students who answer other questions but not this one are from higher-income families. The distribution of non-respondents among the four market segments gives some credibility to this argument.

These four attributes — educational aspirations, parental education, scholastic aptitude, and family income — reflect the basic social patterns of the nation. It would have been surprising if these were not the four social variables that best explained patterns of college choice. Yet the importance of the attributes lies as much in their collective impact as in their individual effect on the student's behavior. Indeed, we come closest to understanding the process of college choice when we examine the interactive effect of these variables.

As we have seen, no one attribute in and of itself firmly places a student in the national segment, but local and in-state students are most often those without any of the four attributes. Table 3.3 asks, "What happens when a student has two attributes or three or all four?" The answer clearly is that the number of attributes makes a great deal of difference. One could be 98.8 percent certain, for example, that a student with all four attributes would not concentrate on local institutions. Indeed, among these 1,201 students, there was an 85-percent chance that they would look outside their home states, focusing largely on the private institutions that dominate regional and national market seg-

Table 3.3. Distribution of Students by Number of Attributes

Number of Attributes	Local	In-State	Regional/National	Number of Students
		Percent*		
0	19.6	45.0	35.3	29,255
1	11.6	38.2	50.2	21,575
2	4.8	28.4	66.8	10,540
3	2.5	18.6	78.9	4,234
4	1.2	13.6	85.1	1,201
Number of Students	8,869	25,365	32,571	66,805
Percent of Total Re-sponding**	13.3	35.0	48.7	100.0

* For students with the given number of attributes, the percentages refer to the proportion classified as local, in-state, or regional/national.
** Students with a missing response on any of the attributes are excluded from this table.

ments. Having three attributes produced nearly the same results: a 97.5-percent chance the students would not belong to the local market segment and a 78.9 percent chance that they would concentrate on regional and national institutions. Thus, Table 3.3 shows a clear and predominant ordering: except in the case of no attributes, all the cells increase in size left to right. The local and in-state entries decrease as the number of attributes increases, while precisely the opposite is true for the combined regional/national category.

It turns out that there is a further ordering to the attributes. We can say with some confidence that the most important single attribute for identifying regional and national students is a high SAT score, followed by college-educated parents, high family income, and post-baccalaureate aspirations. Table 3.4 arrays each of the sixteen possible combinations of attributes in ascending order and notes the percentage of students in each segment (local, in-state, and combined regional/ national) with the given combination of attributes. For the local segment, the percentages generally decrease from top to bottom, with only four relatively minor exceptions. The percentages for the in-state segment also decrease, with only two exceptions. The ordering for regional/ national students is reversed — the percentages increase, with only three exceptions.

It is hard to overemphasize the importance of this statistical pattern. Social data seldom line up as we expect; we are constantly settling for close approximations or suggestive estimation. The information derived from the Market Segment Model, however, is a remarkably

Table 3.4. Distribution of Students by Combinations of Attributes

Attributes		Percent*			
Number	Combination	Local	In-State	Regional/ National	Total
0	None	19.6	45.0	35.3	29,255
1	Seeks more than B.A.	13.2	40.6	46.2	12,814
	Family income ≥ $35,000	8.8	36.0	55.2	3,103
	Both parents with B.A.	10.1	33.9	56.0	2,938
	SATS ≥ 1100	9.1	34.3	56.6	2,720
2	More than B.A. + Income ≥ $35,000	4.5	31.5	64.0	1,842
	More than B.A. + Both parents with B.A.	6.9	30.1	63.0	2,254
	More than B.A. + SATS ≥ 1100	4.7	28.3	67.0	3,758
	Income ≥ $35,000 + Both parents with B.A.	3.8	27.5	68.7	1,474
	Income ≥ $35,000 + SATS ≥ 1100	2.4	23.6	74.0	453
	Both parents with B.A. + SATS ≥ 1100	3.7	20.4	75.9	759
3	More than B.A. + Income ≥ $35,000 + Both parents with B.A.	3.5	20.9	75.6	1,323
	More than B.A. + Income ≥ $35,000 + SATS ≥ 1100	1.4	18.5	80.1	805
	More than B.A. + Both parents with B.A. + SATS ≥ 1100	2.4	18.2	79.4	1,641
	Income ≥ $35,000 + Both parents with B.A. + SATS ≥ 1100	1.7	14.0	84.3	465
4	All	1.2	13.6	85.2	1,201

* For students reporting given combinations of attributes, the percentages refer to the proportion classified as local, in-state, or regional/national.

ordered set of data, consistent in its relationships, that reflects the basic social and economic patterning associated with the structure of college choice.

We can further validate these findings with two additional analyses. The first focuses on the slightly more than 10,000 high school seniors in our sample whose geographic aspirations placed them in regional or national segments even though they possessed none of the four basic attributes. Only one variable significantly distinguishes these national and regional students from local and in-state students who also lacked all of the attributes: among the 10,342 national and regional students without any of the four basic attributes, 4,505, or about 44 percent, received a varsity letter in high school. The implication is that intercollegiate athletics, with its highly developed system of recruiting, represents an alternative source of educational mobility, particularly for those students who lack the socioeconomic attributes that normally expand the geographic range of college choice.

We can also extend our analysis by relaxing some of the criteria used to define the four attributes. In Table 3.5 we analyze those students from families in which at least one parent (rather than both) had earned a baccalaureate degree as well as those students who reported their annual family income to be $25,000 or more (as opposed to $35,000) — the classic middle-income family. The two remaining attributes, post-baccalaureate aspirations and SAT scores of at least 1100, remain unchanged. Redefining the basic attributes in this way increases the number of students with all four attributes from 1,201 to 3,487 and reduces the number of students without any of the four attributes from 29,255 to 18,137. Although this shift toward a more inclusive definition of parental education and family income reduces the statistical clarity of Table 3.3, it offers practical advantages to admissions officers and educational leaders who seek to estimate the limits of their natural applicant pools.

Table 3.5. Distribution of Students by Number of Revised Attributes*

| Number of Attributes | Percent** | | | Number of Students |
	Local	In-State	Regional/National	
0	22.8	45.3	31.9	18,137
1	14.9	42.0	43.1	19,807
2	8.2	35.5	56.3	16,180
3	4.3	27.1	68.6	9,194
4	1.7	17.0	81.3	3,487
Number of Students	8,869	25,365	32,571	66,805
Percent of Total Responding	13.3	35.0	48.7	100.0

* Revised attributes are:
  Seeks more than a B.A.
  Either parent with a B.A.
  SAT (V + M) $\geq$ 1100
  Family income $\geq$ $25,000

** For students with the given number of attributes, the percentages refer to the proportion classified as local, in-state, or regional/national.

Thus far, we have concentrated on aggregate data, which paint a general picture of college choice. What happens if we repeat the analysis for a representative selection of individual markets. Does the correlation between socioeconomic attributes and market segments hold true for every community? The nine sample communities we have selected to test this hypothesis include most of New England's major urban centers, for a total of 40,638 students, or 42 percent of the total New England sample.

Continuing the methodology of the aggregate analysis, Table 3.6 compares socioeconomic attributes and geographic aspirations for the nine markets. Ranging from Boston to Fairfield County, the markets are arranged in ascending order according to the percentage of students in each community reporting two or more of our selected attributes. The bottom row of the table reports the percentage of regional/national students in each market. At first glance, the same left-to-right ordering we have been observing on an aggregate level seems to prevail because the percentages of regional/national students range from a low of 23.0 in Boston to a high of 75.6 in Fairfield County. Two significant exceptions, however, break the familiar pattern. In Springfield, Massachusetts, and in the Malden-Lexington-Waltham suburbs of Boston, the percentages of regional/national students (39.1 and 41.4, respectively) fall far short of what we would expect given the position of these markets in the attribute ordering. Despite its rank as the second most affluent community in our set of nine, the Boston suburbs market is third from the bottom in terms of its proportion of regional and national students. The only two sample communities with lower proportions are the other Massachusetts markets, Boston and Springfield. How can we account for these deviations from the general statistical pattern?

In part, the answer lies in an understanding of statewide educational culture. The New England state most successful in containing within its boundaries the aspirations of most of its own high school seniors is the Commonwealth of Massachusetts. Nearly two out of every three students from Massachusetts concentrate their college choices among Massachusetts institutions (Table 3.7). No other New England state contains even half of its high school seniors within its local and in-state markets. Maine, with its widespread network of university campuses, small number of students, and lagging economy, holds 45.9 percent; and Rhode Island, with its strong localized market around Providence and the University of Rhode Island, holds 40.4 percent of its high school seniors in its local and in-state markets. The remaining three states—Vermont, Connecticut, and New Hampshire—

Table 3.6. Socioeconomic Attributes and Geographic Aspirations of Students from Nine Sample Markets

Sample Market	Boston, MA	Providence, RI	Augusta, ME	Springfield, MA	Manchester, NH	Hartford, CT	Burlington, VT	Malden- Lexington- Waltham, MA	Fairfield County, CT
Percent of Students with Two or More Attributes	14.0	18.8	19.1	20.8	25.0	26.1	29.0	34.4	40.0
Average Number of Attributes Per Student	0.7	0.8	0.7	0.8	0.9	1.0	1.0	1.2	1.3
Percent of Students Classified as Regional or National	23.0	56.2	53.6	39.1 ↑	68.7	68.2	63.4	41.4 ↑	75.6

Note: Markets are arranged in ascending order according to the percentage of students in each community reporting two or more attributes.

Table 3.7. Distribution of Students by State

State	Number of Students	Percent		
		Local/In-State	Regional	National
Massachusetts	48,508	63.2	15.5	21.3
Maine	6,696	45.9	32.8	21.3
Rhode Island	7,016	40.4	36.7	22.9
Vermont	3,211	32.9	32.8	34.3
Connecticut	25,172	30.5	28.5	41.0
New Hampshire	5,965	29.5	40.5	30.0
Total	96,568	48.7	23.7	27.5

hold about 30 percent of their high school students within their re-
spective state markets.

The strength of Massachusetts's internal market is testament both
to the geographic scale of the commonwealth and to its rich variety of
institutions. With its 137 separate institutions, Massachusetts is a major
importer of college students. The dominance of the within-state markets also reflects the strong influence of large private colleges and universities within Massachusetts in general and the Boston area in particular. In many ways, these large institutions, despite their substantial
tuitions, play quasi-public roles in helping distribute students among
the commonwealth's institutions of higher education. In contrast, Connecticut presents a much different picture. Rich in students with high
aspirations and the economic means to pursue them, Connecticut has
not only fewer, but also substantially smaller, institutions of higher
education than Massachusetts. For each of the remaining states, there
is a slightly different mix of basically the same factors: the scale and
scope of within-state institutions, the proportion of population in
urban centers, the relative affluence of the state's dominant communities, and the presence or absence of very large private institutions.

In Table 3.8 we have altered the ordering of our nine sample communities to reflect the special character of Massachusetts markets. The
three Massachusetts markets are grouped separately; otherwise, the
ordering of communities matches the attribute-based progression of
Table 3.6. The percentages of regional/national students now trace a
much clearer, though still imperfect, pattern, rising from a low of 23
percent in Boston (where students possessed the lowest average number of attributes) to a high of 75.6 percent in Fairfield County (where
students possessed the greatest average number of attributes), with
deviations of fewer than 5 percentage points. Considering the three

Table 3.8. Distribution of Students by Nine Sample Markets

		Percent		
Sample Market	*Number of Students*	*Local*	*In-State*	*Regional/ National*
Boston, MA	6,794	42.8	34.2	23.0
Springfield, MA	4,294	38.3	22.6	39.1
Malden-Lexington-Waltham, MA	4,339	1.4	57.2	41.4
Providence, RI	5,096	35.8	8.0	56.2
Augusta, ME	2,465	2.6	43.8	53.6
Manchester, NH	2,403	10.0	21.2	68.7
Hartford, CT	7,058	13.0	18.8	68.2
Burlington, VT	1,010	25.0	11.6	63.4
Fairfield County, CT	7,179	7.7	16.7	75.6

Massachusetts markets as a separate set, the correlation between geographic aspirations and socioeconomic attributes remains in evidence.

Table 3.8 also illustrates the role of specifically local, as opposed to statewide, forces. Boston, Springfield, Providence, and Burlington all have significantly large percentages of students classified as local. Local markets thrive in urban areas where there is an abundant supply of colleges and universities seeking traditional-age students. Table 3.9 confirms that each of these four communities has within its boundaries institutions whose freshman spaces collectively exceed the community's population of college-bound high school graduates. At the other end of the spectrum, the small number of freshman spaces in Augusta could account for this community's poor showing in the local segment (2.6 percent).

In those markets where the local segment is active, the general patterns we have been observing may be magnified on the one hand or complicated on the other. For Boston, the intense local activity simply reinforces the within-state phenomenon we already have noted: low attribute averages, small regional/national component, strong local and in-state segments. In two cases—Springfield and Burlington—the local factor explains anomalies in the general pattern linking social attributes to market segments. As we have seen, Springfield's regional/national percentage is smaller than expected given that city's relatively high position in the attribute ordering. The presence of numerous local options, in conjunction with the many other institutional offerings in Massachusetts, helps to explain this deviation. In the case of Burlington, the anomaly is less pronounced, but the rationale is the same. The market's high attribute level leads us to expect a higher proportion of

Table 3.9. Community Profiles for Nine Sample Markets

Sample Market	Number of Classifiable Test Takers in Market	Number of Institutions	Estimated Freshman Spaces	Freshman Spaces/ Test Takers in Market
Boston, MA	6,794	35	20,800	3.06
Springfield, MA	4,294	14	10,130	2.36
Malden-Lexington-Waltham, MA	4,339	10	4,750	1.09
Providence, RI	5,096	7	6,250	1.23
Augusta, ME	2,465	6	1,610	0.65
Manchester, NH	2,403	10	1,850	0.77
Hartford, CT	7,058	12	4,915	0.70
Burlington, VT	1,010	5	3,100	3.07
Fairfield County, CT	7,179	9	3,325	0.46

regional/national students than its actual percentage of 63.4. Again, local forces, principally the presence of the University of Vermont at Burlington, have complicated the pattern.

Thus, despite the compelling consistency of our aggregate New England analysis, at the community level there can be no simple translation of social attributes into institutional preferences. Even as the data for our nine sample markets confirm the existence of a broadly based socioeconomic ordering, they also testify to a wide range of particular circumstances that represent the community contribution to the structure of college choice. These community influences introduce irregularity and individualism into what might otherwise be perceived as a single sweeping pattern. If we began, then, with an impression of uniformity, we end with an appreciation of linkage. In part, our research has simply demonstrated what everyone has always known: communities with high levels of family income and parental education are also communities in which students have higher than average SATS and more far-reaching aspirations. The logic of cause and effect is here so intertwined that we travel a seamless loop, viewing first one and then another of the three faces—personal, familial, societal—of college choice. By studying one, we can conjure the outlines of the others, but the three never come into focus simultaneously.

Though certain to remain an imperfect mirror, the Market Segment Model can function admirably as an organizational tool. In Figure 3.1 we summarize much of the information that has gone before. Using the same two-tier ordering of Table 3.8, Massachusetts markets versus others, we report both the proportion and the volume of regional/ national students within each community who possess fewer than two, or two or more, of the four basic socioeconomic attributes. Imagine for the moment that you recruit for a college that draws most of its students from regional or national segments. Where would you concentrate your energies? Ideally, you would seek communities with a high proportion of students already predisposed toward institutions such as your own. The Market Segment Model would provide this information through segment percentages for the community in question. Further classification of students by social attributes allows you to identify a group for mailings or recruiting. The volume measurement tells you whether the potential gain in enrollment is worth the cost in energy and resources. Thus, if you were to recruit in Boston, only about two out of every ten students with fewer than two attributes would likely listen, while slightly less than half of the students with two or more attributes would be receptive. If you succeeded in contacting and convincing the 18 percent of the former group and the 47 percent of the latter, you could stand to gain 1,044 students, but at the cost of "wasting" time and

Figure 3.1. Recruiting Targets for Regional and National Students from Nine Sample Markets

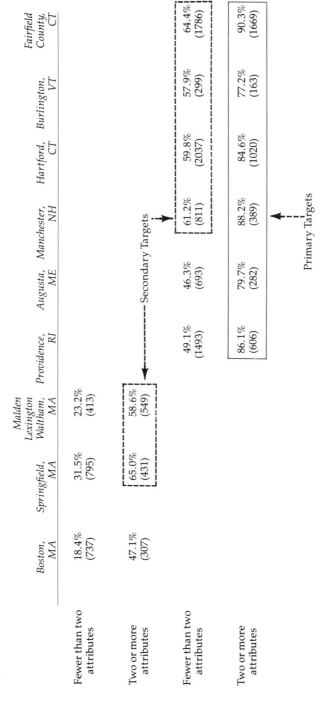

	Boston, MA	Springfield, MA	Malden Lexington Waltham, MA	Providence, RI	Augusta, ME	Manchester, NH	Hartford, CT	Burlington, VT	Fairfield County, CT
Fewer than two attributes	18.4% (737)	31.5% (795)	23.2% (413)						
Two or more attributes	47.1% (307)	65.0% (431)	58.6% (549)						
Fewer than two attributes				49.1% (1493)	46.3% (693)	61.2% (811)	59.8% (2037)	57.9% (299)	64.4% (1786)
Two or more attributes				86.1% (606)	79.7% (282)	88.2% (389)	84.6% (1020)	77.2% (163)	90.3% (1669)

Secondary Targets

Primary Targets

Note: Numbers in parentheses are regional and national students with the specified numbers of attributes; percentages are these students as proportions of all classifiable students in the market with these attributes.

energy on a great many more. Your efforts would surely be better directed toward three of the four communities in the bottom band, Manchester, Hartford, and Fairfield County. Simply by knowing a little bit about the students' backgrounds and academic records you could quickly focus your attention on those most likely to consider your kind of institution. Indeed, in Fairfield County alone you could reach more than 40 percent of your "primary target" population — that is, students with a greater than 75-percent probability of concentrating their college choices among institutions like your own.

What Figure 3.1 provides is a numerical analog to the basic recruiting map most admissions officers intuitively carry with them as part of their admissions kits. On occasion, senior spokespersons for the profession worry that students outside the main market areas remain forgotten and hence, unchallenged. Inevitably, the increasing competition for students, the expense of travel and mailings, and internal political constraints compel institutions to concentrate their efforts where they will do the most good. The result is a natural reinforcing of the basic socioeconomic patterns that gave shape in the first place to the structure of college choice.

We suspect that some people will be distressed by our findings. In the America of the 1980s, they may want to argue, college choice should no longer be a function of family income, parental education, and scholastic aptitude as measured by the SAT; rather, the students' personal ambitions and preferences should determine the kinds of institutions they consider in making this life-defining decision. We are aware, as well, that the rules of statistical inference caution against imputing causal relationships to mere statistical associations. We cannot be sure that the attributes upon which we have focused do, in fact, propel students in particular directions. Our own experiences, our conversations with admissions officers, and the data we have derived from the Market Segment Model, however, all point to a single conclusion: the patterns of college choice are stitched deeply into the social and economic fabric of the nation.

Notes

1. Larry H. Litten, Daniel Sullivan, and David L. Brodigan, *Applying Market Research in College Admissions*, (New York: The College Board, 1983).

2. Most students designate an initial set of institutions to receive their SAT scores before learning how they actually performed on the test. It is only after the student adds institutions to his or her choice set, presumably after learning the results of the examination, that there could be a direct link between the student's range of options and the SAT itself.

4

The Company We Keep: Colleges and Their Competition

If students are aware of the social patterning that so often underlies their college choices, they seldom talk about it except to note, "My friends and I are considering the same kind of schools." Students talk in shorthand phrases about different types of colleges, classifying them on the basis of similarly perceived offerings and settings. Most admissions officers, even most presidents and provosts, intuitively understand that students think not so much of individual institutions as of groups of institutions. In the words of one veteran dean of admissions, "We are known primarily by the company we keep."

For this reason, colleges actually encourage competition with one another to define their places in the market. Members of the Consortium on Financing Higher Education (COFHE) — a group of thirty highly selective, high-cost, private institutions — regularly exchange detailed and confidential information about their applicant pools, admissions strategies, and financial aid programs. What every envious admissions officer outside the Consortium understands is that these thirty institutions are strengthened by their very collectivity, though they are in fact one another's principal competitors. The dean of admissions at one COFHE institution knows that there is greater chance of interesting a student who is already considering another COFHE institution than a student who is not.[1] The same kind of forces help define collective markets for state colleges, women's colleges, Catholic or other church-related institutions, and even diverse urban institutions that share intense athletic rivalries.

While these competitive groupings frequently cut across markets, they clearly vary by market segment. As we have seen, the Market Segment Profile reveals an inherent ordering to institutional competition as well as to the social and economic profiles of the students in each market segment. In our sample market of Fairfield County, Connecticut (see Figure 4.1), the local segment in 1980 was the most concentrated as well as mixed in terms of the types of competing institutions. The in-state market was larger, slightly less concentrated, and clearly more dominated by public institutions. The regional market segment was again larger, involved more institutions and, at the top, was dominated by institutions ranging from public flagship universities to large, private New England institutions. Finally, the national market segment was the largest and included four private institutions among its top five.

In the following discussion, we will analyze in greater detail the variation in competitive patterns from one segment to another, in a single market and statewide. To place these variations in perspective, we then combine data for the different segments, considering the New England region as a whole. On the basis of this analysis, we draw a fundamental conclusion about the structure of college choice: collegiate competition occurs principally between like institutions. As we shall see, the exceptions to this rule are as revealing as the principle itself.

To preserve the anonymity of competing institutions, we have developed a typology based in part on the Carnegie Commission's 1973 classification of colleges and universities (Table 4.1).[2] First we divide the institutions receiving test scores from high school seniors into two sectors — public and private/independent. Both sectors are further divided into three broad categories: flagship institutions (i.e., major research universities), other four-year institutions, and two-year institutions. In the public sector, the flagship category refers to the most complex public institution from each state. The public flagships in New England, for example, are the University of Connecticut at Storrs, the University of Massachusetts at Amherst, the University of Rhode Island, the University of Vermont, the University of New Hampshire, and the University of Maine at Orono. When analyzing the competitive patterns for a particular market, we specify in-state or out-of-state for public flagships. The second broad category within the public sector, four-year institutions other than flagships, refers to state colleges and to four-year branches of the state university system. Finally, the third

Figure 4.1 Sample Market Segment Profile
Connecticut Market 3: Fairfield County

Test Score Submissions

	Local			In-State			Regional			National		
	No.	%	Type	No.	%	Type	No.	%	Type	No.	%	Type
1.	277	50.4	3	757	63.1	2*	610	36.7	2*	1226	32.6	2*
2.	261	47.5	3	515	43.0	3*	348	20.9	2	371	9.9	2
3.	183	33.3	3	438	36.5	3*	272	16.3	2	327	8.7	1
4.	103	18.7	2*	183	15.3	3*	248	14.9	2*	312	8.3	2
5.	100	18.2	3*	177	14.8	3*	197	11.8	2*	308	8.2	2

	Local	In-State	Regional	National
No. of institutions at 5 percent:	11	12	24	17
Percent of all scores going to 5 percent institutions:	84.3	69.6	51.2	26.8

Student Descriptors

	Local	In-State	Regional	National
Total test takers:	550	1,199	1,664	3,766
Average SAT (V+M):	770	850	970	980
Average # scores per test taker:	2.8	3.5	4.8	5.3
Self-Reported				
Percent in top quintile:	27.8	26.1	44.7	45.7
% aspiring to more than B.A.:	30.6	41.5	54.5	62.2
% family income more than $35,000:	11.2	20.6	41.9	43.0
% both parents with B.A.:	9.0	16.3	34.0	37.1

Legend for Institutional Type
* = public
1 = major research university
2 = doctoral-granting university
3 = comprehensive college
4 = liberal arts college
5 = two-year institution
6 = other

Table 4.1. Classification of Institutions

	Public	Private
Flagship Institutions	In-state major research universities Out-of-state major research universities	Major research universities
Other Four-Year Institutions	State colleges Nonflagship university campuses	Selective colleges and universities Standard colleges and universities Linking colleges and universities
Two-Year Institutions	Community or junior colleges Technical or vocational colleges	Junior colleges Technical or vocational colleges

category, public two-year institutions, includes community and junior colleges as well as technical and vocational colleges.

In the private sector, flagships are those institutions classified by the Carnegie Commission as major research universities. The second category, private four-year institutions, is further divided into three subgroups that reflect a considerable range of institutions in terms of both scale and mission.[3] The first subgroup, selective colleges and universities, consists of those four-year colleges and nonflagship universities that compete in the private sector's high-cost/high-ability student market. Such institutions charge substantial tuitions (in 1980, more than $5,400) and seek students with high grade point averages and high SAT scores.[4] The second subgroup, standard colleges and universities, refers to other four-year private institutions that charge lower tuitions, are more likely to practice broad or open admissions, and are more likely to seek commuter students and adult learners. The third subgroup, linking colleges and universities, is unique in our typology by virtue of its specialized definition. In New England, this subgroup includes only four institutions, two urban and two Catholic institutions located in Massachusetts. In the regional segment of markets across New England, each of these four private institutions often provides a link between the public and private sectors by competing with both types of institutions. In different segments of different markets, other categories of institutions may play this role, but none so consistently as this type in the regional segment.[5] Finally, the third broad category of institutions in the private sector, two-year colleges, is composed of junior colleges and technical or vocational colleges.

Using these institutional types, we come at last to the Tinker Toys. The schematics, or Tinker Toy diagrams, displayed in Figures 4.2 through 4.5 detail institutional competition in each segment of our sample market of Fairfield County. A line connecting two institutions signifies a reciprocal competitive relationship. Specifically, such a line means that 15 percent of the students who sent SAT scores to the first institution also sent a score to the second and that 15 percent of the students who sent an SAT score to the second institution also sent one to the first. The number in each box identifies that institution's competitive rank for that market segment as measured by the volume of students submitting SAT scores.[6]

Figure 4.2 portrays the competitive structure of the local market of Fairfield County—a simple, highly concentrated market segment. In the upper half of the diagram are the four top-ranked institutions—two Catholic standard colleges located in Fairfield County, a nonsectarian private standard college also located in Fairfield County, and the state's public flagship. The most frequently named institution, and in that sense the most visible to local students, is a Catholic standard college, while the public flagship is the fourth most visible institution. Together these four institutions comprise a competitive "quad" in which each institution overlaps with the other three. Collectively, this competitive quad accounts for just over half the market activity generated by the 550 local students in Fairfield County.

Attached to the fourth-ranked public flagship, which in fact has a branch within Fairfield County, are three public institutions: one of Connecticut's state colleges, a community college located in Fairfield County, and a two-year specialized technical school also located in Fairfield County. This two-year college, in turn, has a competitive relationship with a second two-year technical institution. A detached set of nursing programs is followed by a string of apparently dissimilar institutions: a community college, a second state college, and finally, a private standard college located outside of Fairfield County.

This competition structure for the local market of Fairfield County is typical in four respects of competitive patterns in local market segments. First, it is within local markets that competition is sharpest between public and private institutions. Second, the local Catholic institutions play a critical role in structuring competition within local markets.[7] Third, despite the fact that community colleges do not require SAT scores, their positions in the market can be clearly identified, though their competitive ranks as measured by volume of scores are

50

Figure 4.2. Structure of Fairfield County Local Market

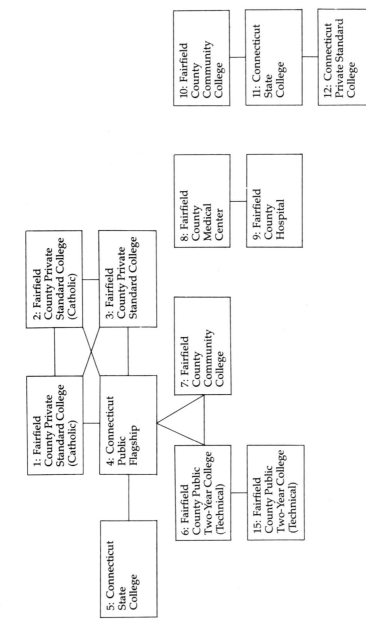

Note: Connecting lines indicate reciprocal competitive overlap of ≥ 15 percent.

understated. Finally, local market segments tend to be highly concentrated: in Fairfield County, only eleven institutions account for about 84 percent of the total local market activity (see Figure 4.1).

The in-state segment of Fairfield County exhibits a comparable degree of concentration and simplicity (Figure 4.3). At the top of the structure is the in-state public flagship. Ranked number one in terms of volume, it receives a test score from nearly two of every three in-state students from Fairfield County. Attached to the in-state public flagship is a competitive quad consisting of the four state colleges, though only two are directly competitive with the in-state flagship. Collectively, these five institutions account for just under 50 percent of the market activity of in-state students in Fairfield County. The remaining scores go first to a loosely connected set of six private standard colleges, including the two Catholic institutions in Fairfield County that topped the competition for local students. These six institutions collectively account for 16 percent of the in-state students' activity. Finally, there is a small but important set of selective institutions—a private flagship and three private selective colleges—that form a competitive set at the periphery of the market structure.

The most striking feature of the in-state market structure is its clearly defined layering of public and private competition, beginning with a public sector in which the in-state public flagship plays the dominant role. Next comes a group of private colleges and universities that, for the most part, are attractive both to local and in-state students. The final layer is composed of several selective private institutions that are often grouped together in the college choice sets of a small but discernible group of in-state students who want to remain near home while enrolling at a high-cost/high-ability institution. There are no links across the three layers, and no non-Connecticut institutions appear.

When we turn to the regional segment of Fairfield County, we leave simplicity, though not order, behind (Figure 4.4). Embedded in the upper competition set is Connecticut's public flagship. As the top-ranked institution, it receives a test score from one of every three regional students in Fairfield County. The flagship is part of two nearly complete competitive quads. Accounting for a third of the total market activity generated by regional students in Fairfield County, the upper quad links Connecticut's public flagship with three out-of-state New England institutions—a public flagship and two private linking colleges, including one of the two Catholic institutions that play this special role of bridging competition between public and private sectors.

Figure 4.3. Structure of Fairfield County In-State Market

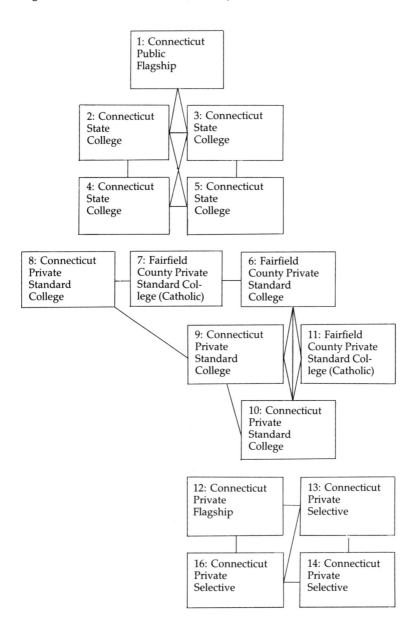

Note: Connecting lines indicate reciprocal competitive overlap of ≥ 15 percent.

Figure 4.4. Structure of Fairfield County Regional Market

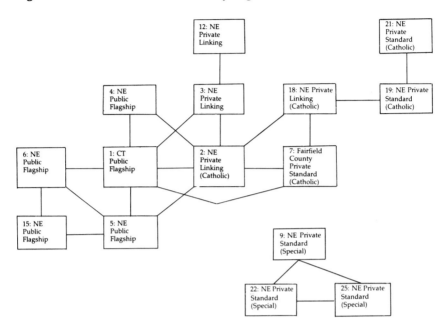

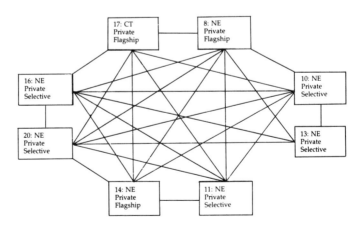

Note: Connecting lines indicate reciprocal competitive overlap of ≥ 15 percent.

Significantly, all four linking institutions are part of the regional market structure in Fairfield County, with the two Catholic links anchoring the Catholic portion of the private college market. Except for the overlap between the in-state public flagship and the Fairfield County Catholic institution, itself a carryover from the local market structure, all competition between public and private institutions in the regional segment passes through one of these linking institutions. The incomplete quad extending to the left of the in-state public flagship consists of the other three out-of-state public flagships.

The remaining competition for regional students in this market is taken up by two highly distinct sets of colleges and universities. First is a group of eight high-cost/high-ability private institutions—three private flagships (one located in Connecticut) and five selective New England colleges. The competitive overlap among these eight is nearly complete. Only the thirteenth-ranked institution lacks a competitive relationship with three of the others, which are, in fact, larger institutions.[8] The second distinct set of institutions is a triad of private New England standard colleges with highly specialized reputations and curricula (in this case, business).

The significance of the market structure set forth in Figure 4.4 may be simply stated: the principal competition for regional students is among like institutions. Public institutions compete principally with other public institutions, while private institutions compete with other private institutions. Only the four linking institutions in this regional market (as well as in most other regional markets) offer substantial competition to both public and private institutions. Competitive overlap, moreover, is often confined to institutions belonging to the same type as well as sector. For example, public flagships compete primarily with other public flagships; private standard colleges, with other private standard colleges; Catholic institutions, with other Catholic institutions. Only in the case of the high-cost/high-ability market do we find a significant exception to this general rule, as private flagships overlap with private selective colleges. Despite their difference in scale, these two types of institutions share a commonality of price and program at the undergraduate level.

The patterns we have been observing in the regional segment are carried over and further developed in the national segment of the Fairfield County market, in which almost all competition is among private institutions (Figure 4.5). The most conspicuous feature of the national market structure is a circle of eight highly selective, high-cost private institutions, seven of which are private flagships. Half of the circle consists of New England institutions, while the other half is composed of

Figure 4.5. Structure of Fairfield County National Market

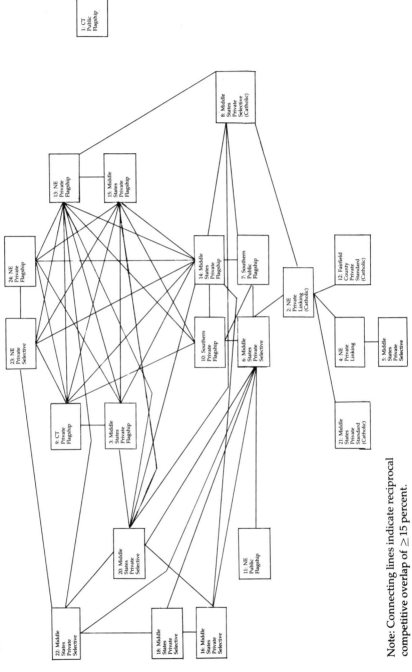

Note: Connecting lines indicate reciprocal competitive overlap of ≥ 15 percent.

three Middle States private flagships and a private flagship in the South. An outer ring of institutions is drawn from the private, high-cost/high-ability market, except for two public flagships, one located within New England and the other in the South.

The key institution in the market, however, as measured by volume of scores received, lies outside this structure. The first-named institution is Connecticut's public flagship, which again received a test score from one of every three national students in Fairfield County (see Figure 4.1). Significantly, the public flagship is not paired with any other institution, suggesting that in this market segment, it is more an alternative choice than a member of a set. Put simply, the in-state public flagship, despite its heavy draw from the national market, does not appear to keep company with the selective private institutions that, in fact, structure competition for nationally oriented Fairfield County students. Indeed, of the five top-ranked institutions, only the third, the Middle States private flagship, is embedded in the structure. The second-ranked and fourth-ranked institutions, which in the regional market provided a critical linking function, similarly lie largely outside the prime circle of competition, despite the volume of scores they received.

The national segment of Fairfield County thus conforms in almost every sense to the classic description of competition among the three dozen or so institutions that traditionally have sought nationally oriented students within New England. Few admissions officers would not be able to name the eight institutions comprising the inner circle of this competition structure. Most observers of eastern colleges would be correct most of the time if they attempted to name the institutions in the outer circle. The standard stories about college competition in this segment of the admissions market simply are true. There is, in fact, a clearly defined group of institutions that shape public perceptions of selective educational options. Though individually ranked lower in some cases than other institutions, these colleges and universities collectively dominate the high-cost/high-ability market.

Our schematic representations of the four segments of the Fairfield County market typify the configuration of markets across New England and in much of the eastern third of the United States. Local markets involve only a few institutions, all in intense competition with one another. These competitive patterns, unlike those in the other three segments, regularly cross boundaries of institutional sector and type. Public flagships, for example, often compete directly with private standard colleges as well as with state colleges and community colleges. In-state market structures, however, tend to be layered, the public and private competition sets operating independently of one another. These markets are dominated by public institutions: at the core is the in-state public flagship, which overlaps with other campuses or branches of the state university system and with the state's public colleges. The private sector of most in-state markets consists of two components: a relatively small group of private selective institutions and a group of private standard colleges that includes Catholic and urban institutions within the state. Regional markets also have two centers, but the division between public and private is less sharp, for the four linking institutions bridge the gap between public institutions and private standard colleges. The nation's leading private institutions, however, function as a second independent competition set. Finally, in the national market segment these selective private institutions move to the forefront, their entwined competition forming what looks like a complex ball of yarn.

Statewide data on competitive overlap by market segment show the influence of local variations even as they confirm the general patterns traced in the Fairfield County market. Tables 4.2 through 4.6 display competitive profiles for seven sample institutions, reporting their total draw from local, in-state, regional, and national market segments in the Commonwealth of Massachusetts.[9] Six of the seven sample institutions are located in Massachusetts, thus highlighting the in-state segment. The data include the number of scores received by the institution from each segment, the total number of scores these students sent to other institutions, and the average number of scores per test taker. The percentage distribution of overlapping scores is recorded for each of the six broad categories in our institutional typology: public and private flagships, public and private four-year institutions, public and private two-year institutions.

Table 4.2 details the statewide competition of a private flagship located in Massachusetts. This institution received scores from 3,219 Massachusetts high school seniors: 41 percent from in-state students, 32 percent from national students, 18 percent from regional students, and just under 9 percent from local students. Most, indeed nearly 85 percent, of this private flagship's competition comes from other private institutions. In the regional and national markets, we see a clear separation between competition with other private flagships (15.5 percent and 44.4 percent) and with public four-year institutions (1.1 percent and 0.5 percent). Note the extent to which this institution's national, but not its regional, competition is with other private flagship institutions. Many of these private flagships are New England institutions, confirming the singular importance of just a handful of private flagship universities in the competition for national students.[10]

The competition profile for our sample private selective college (Table 4.3), also located in Massachusetts, is much the same as that for our sample private flagship. Again we see the particular strength of the

Table 4.2. Statewide Competition for Private Flagship

				Percentage Distribution of Overlapping Scores			
				Flagship	Other Four-Year	Two-Year	Total
Segment: Local							
Number of Scores Received	283	Public		4.4	10.2	0.6	15.2
Number of Overlapping Scores	1,022	Private		11.1	69.2	4.6	84.8
Average Scores/Test Taker	4.6	Total		15.5	79.4	5.2	XXXX
Segment: In-State							
Number of Scores Received	1,308	Public		9.8	8.7	0.6	19.1
Number of Overlapping Scores	5,221	Private		6.9	68.4	5.7	80.9
Average Scores/Test Taker	5.0	Total		16.7	77.0	6.3	XXXX
Segment: Regional							
Number of Scores Received	592	Public		11.3	1.1	0.1	12.6
Number of Overlapping Scores	3,035	Private		15.5	71.2	0.8	87.4
Average Scores/Test Taker	6.1	Total		26.8	72.3	0.9	XXXX
Segment: National							
Number of Scores Received	1,036	Public		9.7	0.5	0.9	11.1
Number of Overlapping Scores	4,853	Private		44.4	43.9	0.6	88.9
Average Scores/Test Taker	5.7	Total		54.1	44.4	1.5	XXXX

Table 4.3 Statewide Competition for Private Selective College

			Percentage Distribution of Overlapping Scores			
			Flagship	Other Four-Year	Two-Year	Total
Segment: Local						
Number of Scores Received	105	Public	15.7	12.0	11.7	39.4
Number of Overlapping Scores	325	Private	8.0	43.4	9.2	60.6
Average Scores/Test Taker	4.1	Total	23.7	55.4	20.9	XXXX
Segment: In-State						
Number of Scores Received	772	Public	12.3	20.1	3.1	35.5
Number of Overlapping Scores	2,852	Private	8.6	50.1	5.8	64.5
Average Scores/Test Taker	4.7	Total	20.9	70.1	8.9	XXXX
Segment: Regional						
Number of Scores Received	240	Public	13.1	1.1	0.2	14.3
Number of Overlapping Scores	1,224	Private	17.6	67.6	0.6	85.7
Average Scores/Test Taker	6.1	Total	30.6	68.6	0.7	XXXX
Segment: National						
Number of Scores Received	233	Public	10.3	0.2	0.7	11.2
Number of Overlapping Scores	963	Private	37.5	50.7	0.6	88.8
Average Scores/Test Taker	5.1	Total	47.8	50.9	1.3	XXXX

in-state market in Massachusetts, which causes an unusually high over-lap (20.1 percent) between public four-year institutions and our sample selective college in the in-state segment. In the regional and national segments, however, the sample college competes primarily with other private institutions, private flagships again playing a major role in or-ganizing the competition for national students.

To depict patterns of competition for private standard colleges, we have developed a composite of several institutions. The upper band of Table 4.4 reports the competition for a largely commuter institution that received only fifteen scores from regional students and none from national students. Roughly two-thirds of the students interested in this institution came from in-state markets, and the other third came from the institution's local Boston market, where competition for local stu-dents was predominantly private (66.2 percent), reflecting the generally private range of options available in the Boston area. In the in-state market, however, this private institution drew a little over 44 percent of its competition from public colleges and universities. While its domi-nant competition was still with other private institutions like itself, nearly one of every three options developed by students interested in this college was in the public sector.

The middle band of Table 4.4 reports the in-state competition for a small women's college in Massachusetts. Its problems are simply stated. Of the nearly 40,000 college-bound high school seniors in Mas-sachusetts, only 146 in-state, 13 local, and 8 regional students sent scores to this institution. Its principal competition was with other, often similarly priced, private institutions. Thus, this college's problem was not price competition from public institutions but lack of sustained visibility for a single-gender college in the 1980s.

The lower band of Table 4.4 details the statewide competition for a flourishing, largely nonselective, private college whose strength lies in its specialized programs. While nearly 85 percent of the students in-terested in this college came from the Massachusetts in-state market, the college nonetheless enjoyed significant local and regional visi-bility. In the local market this college, like its commuter-based neigh-bor, drew almost 70 percent of its competition from other private institutions, principally standard colleges. The same proportion holds true in the regional market. Note, however, that only 2.6 percent of its competition in this segment came from private flagships; nearly a quarter of its competition was from public flagships. In the in-state segment, this private standard college faced even stronger public com-petition: nearly 30 percent of the options developed by its potential students included a four-year public institution.

Table 4.4. Statewide Competition for Three Private Standard Colleges

				Percentage Distribution of Overlapping Scores		
			Flagship	*Other* Four-Year	Two-Year	*Total*
A. Commuter Institution						
Segment: Local						
Number of Scores Received	457	Public	3.6	27.9	2.3	33.8
Number of Overlapping Scores	1,371	Private	4.4	53.5	8.3	66.2
Average Scores/Test Taker	4.0	Total	8.0	81.5	10.6	XXXX
Segment: In-State						
Number of Scores Received	826	Public	8.1	32.7	3.3	44.1
Number of Overlapping Scores	3,328	Private	1.7	44.6	9.6	55.9
Average Scores/Test Taker	5.0	Total	9.8	77.3	12.9	XXXX
B. Women's College						
Segment: In-State						
Number of Scores Received	146	Public	11.6	16.8	0.4	28.7
Number of Overlapping Scores	554	Private	4.9	64.3	2.2	71.3
Average Scores/Test Taker	4.8	Total	16.4	81.0	2.5	XXXX
C. Specialized College						
Segment: Local						
Number of Scores Received	200	Public	3.7	19.8	7.3	30.7
Number of Overlapping Scores	602	Private	3.3	56.3	9.6	69.3
Average Scores/Test Taker	4.0	Total	7.0	76.1	16.9	XXXX
Segment: In-State						
Number of Scores Received	2,368	Public	10.0	29.2	3.7	42.9
Number of Overlapping Scores	8,903	Private	1.4	42.8	12.9	57.1
Average Scores/Test Taker	4.6	Total	11.4	72.0	16.6	XXXX
Segment: Regional						
Number of Scores Received	275	Public	24.1	8.2	1.0	33.3
Number of Overlapping Scores	1,024	Private	2.6	41.4	22.7	66.7
Average Scores/Test Taker	4.7	Total	26.8	49.6	23.6	XXXX

As an example in the public sector, Table 4.5 profiles a Massachusetts state college. On a local level, over 70 percent of the college's competition is with other public institutions, principally the market's two community colleges. It is in the regional segment that the state college comes closest to facing significant private competition. Over a third of the options developed by the state college's potential students in the regional market are four-year private colleges and universities. For all intents and purposes, the sample institution offers no competition to private flagships.

Nearly 90 percent of this state college's potential students are drawn from the in-state segment. The competition within this segment is predominantly public, with about one of every two options its potential students develop being another state college or a nonflagship state university campus. Here just 3 percent of its competition is with community colleges and less than 15 percent with the state's public flagship. Even four-year private institutions account for less than 25 percent of the options developed by this state college's potential students in the in-state segment. It seems hard to escape the conclusion that for state colleges such as our sample institution, range of offerings, campus settings, and institutional reputations, rather than price, will determine long-term enrollment potential.

We cannot present a competitive overlap profile for the public flagship in Massachusetts, for to do so would violate the confidentiality of the data. Table 4.6, however, does report the competition profile for a neighboring state's public flagship, showing its draw from Massachusetts. The students that this institution attracts from the in-state segment of Massachusetts develop an unusually large number of collegiate options, submitting an average of 5.5 scores as compared to an overall average of 4.6 scores per test taker for all Massachusetts in-state students. As it moves from the in-state market into the regional and national markets, this out-of-state public flagship faces increasing private competition.

In large measure, the overlap data for these seven sample institutions reinforce the lessons drawn from our analysis of competitive structure in the different market segments of Fairfield County. With the exception of the out-of-state public flagship, each of the sample institutions finds its principal competition in its own sector: public vs. public, private vs. private. In several important instances, the overlap data also illustrate the extent to which competition respects boundaries of institutional type. Even with its condensed typology, the analysis shows a private flagship competing with other private flagships, a public four-year college competing with other public four-year col-

Table 4.5. Statewide Competition for State College

				Percentage Distribution of Overlapping Scores			
				Flagship	Other Four-Year	Two-Year	Total
Segment: Local							
Number of Scores Received	126		Public	14.1	22.2	34.1	70.4
Number of Overlapping Scores	270		Private	0.0	24.8	4.8	29.6
Average Scores/Test Taker	3.1		Total	14.0	47.0	38.9	XXXX
Segment: In-State							
Number of Scores Received	2,445		Public	13.4	52.5	3.0	68.9
Number of Overlapping Scores	9,918		Private	0.5	23.5	7.1	31.1
Average Scores/Test Taker	5.1		Total	13.9	76.0	10.2	XXXX
Segment: Regional							
Number of Scores Received	163		Public	29.5	23.1	1.1	53.6
Number of Overlapping Scores	662		Private	1.2	37.5	7.7	46.4
Average Scores/Test Taker	5.1		Total	30.7	60.6	8.8	XXXX

Table 4.6. Statewide Competition for Out-of-State Public Flagship

			Percentage Distribution of Overlapping Scores	Other		
			Flagship	Four-Year	Two-Year	Total
Segment: Local						
Number of Scores Received	50	Public	4.7	21.4	5.7	31.6
Number of Overlapping Scores	192	Private	6.8	56.3	5.2	68.2
Average Scores/Test Taker	4.8	Total	11.5	77.6	10.9	XXXX
Segment: In-State						
Number of Scores Received	1,557	Public	15.0	31.8	1.4	48.2
Number of Overlapping Scores	6,968	Private	2.4	42.5	7.0	51.8
Average Scores/Test Taker	5.5	Total	17.4	74.2	8.4	XXXX
Segment: Regional						
Number of Scores Received	2,266	Public	30.8	9.8	0.6	41.1
Number of Overlapping Scores	8,275	Private	4.1	50.5	4.3	58.9
Average Scores/Test Taker	4.7	Total	34.9	60.2	4.8	XXXX
Segment: National						
Number of Scores Received	748	Public	27.2	3.1	1.6	31.9
Number of Overlapping Scores	2,345	Private	17.4	48.5	2.1	68.1
Average Scores/Test Taker	4.1	Total	44.7	51.6	3.7	XXXX

leges. The analysis also highlights exceptions to this tendency for institutional competition to occur within, rather than across, sectors and types. Mixed competition in local segments, overlap between private selective colleges and private flagships, competition between out-of-state public flagships and private institutions in the national segment— all of these relationships appear in the overlap data, confirming patterns traced in the Fairfield County analysis.

In one respect, however, the overlap data offer a new perspective on the structure of institutional competition. As we have seen, the private standard colleges represented in the overlap analysis find a large, though not dominant, proportion of their competition in the public sector. Several factors are involved in this phenomenon. The first concerns the nature of the data. The Tinker Toy diagrams describe relationships among individual institutions, showing the most visible members of the competition set in a given market segment. The overlap data, however, summarize a sample institution's statewide competition by reporting the total volume of overlapping scores, not for individual institutions but for groups of institutions classified by type, thus broadening the view of institutional competition.[11] In this way, we find that those students sending scores to the sample private standard colleges are at the same time dispersing their interest widely in the public sector. A second consideration is simply the particular character of the three private standard colleges used in our analysis. The sample women's college, like the most visible private standard colleges in Fairfield County, defies the tendency toward public competition exhibited by the commuter and specialized institutions.

Finally, the specific character of the aggregate market in question, the Commonwealth of Massachusetts, strongly influences the configuration of institutional competition. With its rich variety of institutions, public as well as private, Massachusetts offers compelling reasons for students to remain within the commonwealth, creating an exceptionally strong in-state segment in which private standard colleges and public institutions tend to compete head on. In the in-state segment, even our private selective college encountered substantial competition with four-year public institutions. Given this highly competitive educational environment, many private standard colleges in Massachusetts become vulnerable to public competition and must be especially sensitive to price differentials between themselves and Massachusetts' public institutions.

The data we have examined thus far have been disaggregated by market segment, showing changes in competitive patterns from one segment to another, one market to another. Even as we have cata-

Table 4.7. Distribution of Students by Institutional Type

Institutional Type	Number of Institutions	Number of Interested Students	Percent of Total Classified
Total classified students = 84,036 (local segment excluded)			
Private Standard	187	42,149	50.2
Four-Year Public	89	36,763	43.7
In-State Public Flagship	6	31,403	37.4
Private Selective	35	25,999	30.9
Private Linking	4	24,956	29.7
Out-of-State Public Flagship	26	21,399	25.5
Private Flagship	21	16,067	19.1

logued these variations, an underlying structure has continually reasserted itself. When we aggregate the data, combining information for the different segments and the different markets of the region, the contours of that structure emerge with a striking clarity.[12]

Table 4.7 reports the number of classified New England students sending a score to at least one institution of a given type. The single largest group was composed of students interested in private standard colleges. Approximately one of every two New England students was interested in at least one private standard college. Thereafter follow four-year public institutions (43.7 percent), in-state public flagships (37.4 percent), private selective colleges (30.9 percent), private linking institutions (29.7 percent), out-of-state public flagships (25.5 percent), and private flagships (19.1 percent). The striking feature of these data is the relative absence of truly mixed choices. If one of every two students sent a score to a private standard college, it is also true that one of every two students did not develop this particular private option. Nearly six of every ten students were not interested in a state college. Almost two-thirds of the students were not interested in their state's public flagship. Seven of every ten students were not interested in the flagship institution of a neighboring state. Finally, eight of every ten students were not interested in a private flagship.

These constraints are further quantified in the overlap matrix of Table 4.8. As we read down each column, the first entry reports the number of students interested in at least one institution of the type specified by the column heading; the remaining numbers in the column indicate how many of the students interested in that type also expressed interest in each of the other institutional types specified by the row headings. Thus, of the 16,067 students sending a score to at least

Table 4.8. Competitive Overlap by Institutional Type

Institutional Type	Private Flagship	Private Selective	Private Standard	Private Linking	Out-of-State Public Flagship	In-State Public Flagship	Four-Year Public
Private Flagship	16,067						
Private Selective	11,416	25,999					
Private Standard	7,106	14,564	42,149				
Private Linking	5,487	9,646	13,999	24,956			
Out-of-State Public Flagship	5,347	8,771	11,689	7,139	21,399		
In-State Public Flagship	5,068	9,128	15,484	9,713	9,462	31,403	
Four-Year Public	3,602	6,201	17,250	10,662	8,571	14,676	36,763

Note: Data exclude scores received from students in the local segment.

one private flagship, 3,602 also sent a score to at least one public four-year institution. If we convert this to a percentage (3,602 divided by 16,067), we see that only about 22 percent of those students interested in a private flagship were interested in any one of eighty-nine public four-year institutions. Again, the startling feature of the data displayed in Table 4.8 is the relative absence of large overlaps. A single significant exception is the 71.1-percent overlap of private flagships with private selective colleges, a phenomenon noted in our earlier analyses by segment. No other overlap exceeds 55 percent.

These data demonstrate that there is a fundamental compartmentalization of student interest among institutions of the same type, that there is in fact a structure to college choice. Still, as we have seen, under certain conditions the boundaries between institutional types and even sectors are regularly crossed. Using the aggregate data displayed in Table 4.8, we can construct one final Tinker Toy to summarize how and why those connections occur (see Figure 4.6). Here we define significant competition as 42-percent overlap in either direction: either 42 percent of those students interested in institutions of Type A also sent a score to at least one institution of Type B, or 42 percent of those students interested in Type B institutions also sent a score to at least one Type A institution. Noted within each box is the average tuition cost for institutions of that type.

Four of the seven institutional types—private flagships, private selective colleges, private linking institutions, and out-of-state public flagships—exhibit only two connections apiece. For private flagships and private selective colleges, the overlap as defined for this analysis is contained within the private sector, as each overlaps with the other and with private standard colleges. Highlighted in the overlap matrix (Table 4.8) as well as in the regional and national Tinker Toys for Fairfield County (Figures 4.4 and 4.5), the overlap between private flagships and private selective colleges is a natural result of their comparably high tuitions ($5,574 and $5,434 respectively) and common quest for high-ability students. As one would expect, private linking institutions bridge sectors, overlapping with private standard colleges on the one hand and four-year public colleges on the other.[13] Out-of-state public flagships overlap with private standard colleges and with in-state public flagships. As we saw in our analyses of statewide overlap (Table 4.6), public flagships tend to adopt a private guise when acting in their out-of-state capacity. Four-year public institutions exhibit the same two connections, with private standard colleges and in-state public flagships, as well as with private linking colleges.

Two institutional types, in-state public flagships and private stan-

Figure 4.6. Competition Structure by Institutional Type with Average Tuitions

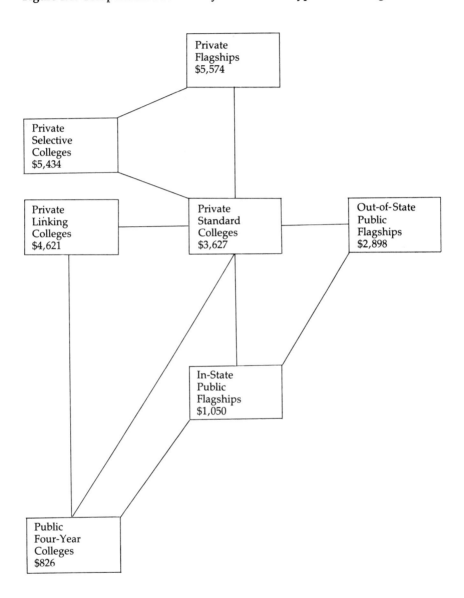

Note: Connecting lines indicate competitive overlap of 42 percent in either direction.

dard colleges, are distinctive for their connections across sectors as well
as types. In-state public flagships overlap with three types — standard
colleges in the private sector, out-of-state flagships and four-year colleges on the public side. In the analysis of Fairfield County, we saw the
in-state public flagship playing different roles in different segments. In
the local segment it overlapped with private standard colleges, in the
local and in-state markets it competed with state colleges, and in the
regional segment it competed with out-of-state public flagships and
private linking institutions. In the national market, it was set apart as
the top-ranked institution in terms of the volume of scores received,
but it failed to meet the criterion of 15-percent reciprocal overlap with
any other single institution. Its influence, in other words, was not concentrated among a specific set of highly visible institutions but dispersed among a broad spectrum of institutions being considered by
national students in Fairfield County. When data for the different segments are combined in our summary Tinker Toy, in-state public flagships may be seen to play a key role in the market as a whole, competing seriously with many institutions of different types and serving
as a backup alternative in the case of many more.

Private standard colleges are even more interwoven into the competition structure. Overlapping with each of the other six institutional
types, they literally compete with everyone. If the private standard colleges collectively have the largest share of the market, just over 50 percent, they are also the most vulnerable to competition based on prestige
and selectivity on the one hand and to competition based on price on
the other. As a hierarchy of price, the Tinker Toy diagram ranges from
private flagships, with an average tuition of $5,574, to public four-year
institutions at $826. With an average tuition of $3,627, private standard
colleges stand in the center of the diagram financially as well as spa-
tially. Unlike their more selective private competitors or their lower-
priced public competitors, many moderately priced private standard
colleges have been unable to establish a unique market of their own.

One final turn completes our analysis. Given the inherent order
that has characterized so much of the data generated by the Market
Segment Model, no one should be surprised that the hierarchical structure of institutional competition is strongly correlated with the socioeconomic attributes students bring to the process of college choice. In
an earlier analysis, we classified students according to four such attributes: (1) Student seeks higher degree than a B.A. (2) Both of student's
parents earned a B.A. (3) Student has combined SAT scores of 1,100 or
more. (4) Student's family income is $35,000 or more.[14] Figure 4.7 re-
peats the Tinker Toy diagram representing competition among and be-

Figure 4.7. Competition Structure by Institutional Type with Average Number of Socioeconomic Attributes*

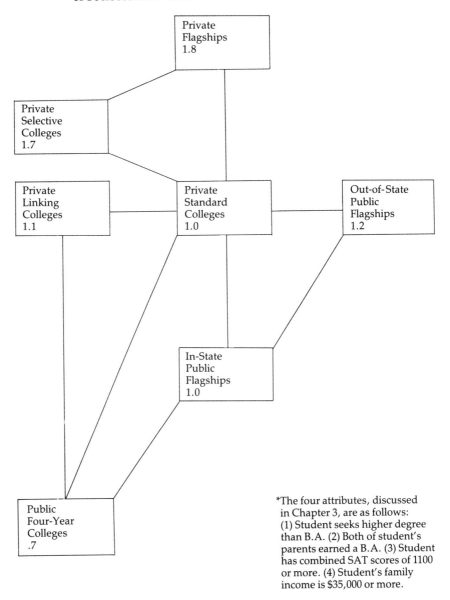

*The four attributes, discussed in Chapter 3, are as follows: (1) Student seeks higher degree than B.A. (2) Both of student's parents earned a B.A. (3) Student has combined SAT scores of 1100 or more. (4) Student's family income is $35,000 or more.

Note: Connecting lines indicate competitive overlap of 42 percent in either direction.

tween the seven institutional types. Noted within each box is the average number of attributes possessed by all students sending at least one score to an institution of the specified type. Thus, on the average, students interested in private flagships possessed 1.8 attributes, while students interested in private selective colleges possessed 1.7. At the other end of the spectrum, students sending scores to public four-year colleges possessed only 0.7 attributes. Generally speaking, the numbers in the boxes, like the average tuitions in Figure 4.6, decrease from top to bottom.

We now know why students so seldom speak of their own social or family backgrounds in explaining how they go about choosing a college. They have no need to. Students describe themselves socially simply by telling us the colleges and universities in which they are interested. The layering of collegiate competition is primarily a socioeconomic layering. The hierarchical structure of collegiate competition largely reflects the stratified social and economic dimensions of the communities from which colleges draw their students. Competition among colleges, as admissions officers have told us for so long, is, in fact, a matter of keeping company with one's peers.

Notes

1. Competition among COFHE institutions is best documented in a set of confidential analyses known both within and without the Consortium as *Redbooks*.

2. As noted in Chapter 2, the Carnegie Commission's 1973 classification of institutions was used in conjunction with the Market Segment Profiles for the 1979–80 cycle of CUEPP data. There then followed a series of regional workshops in which individual institutions analyzed their own data and suggested changes in format and definition. One result was a simplified institutional typology. In this chapter we have taken that new set of definitions one step further by dividing the four-year private category into three subgroups: selective, standard, and linking.

3. To preserve the anonymity of individual institutions, we do not distinguish colleges from universities in the private four-year category. In both text and figures, all selective, standard, or linking institutions are referred to simply as colleges.

4. The average tuition figure cited here was reported in *The College Board Handbook 1980–81* (New York, 1980). Though categorized separately, private flagships as undergraduate institutions also compete in the high-cost/high-ability market. In defining our selective-colleges subgroup, we began with a core group of fourteen private colleges and fifteen private flagships generally recognized as practicing selective admissions. Next, using data from Table 19 of the ATP Round II Report, we noted which colleges and universities overlapped with our core institutions. Specifically, any private four-year college or nonflagship university appearing among the thirty-five institutions most often named overlapping with any two core institutions was included in the selective-colleges subgroup.

5. In the other regions, most noticeably the South, linking institutions are usually public universities with strong out-of-state draws. None, however, assumes an organizing role comparable to that of these four Massachusetts institutions, in part because of the strong Catholic dimension of the New England market.

6. Though significant competition often occurs at a lower threshold than 15 percent, this criterion allows us to focus on the most fundamental competitive relationships in each market segment. We have also limited presentation in each market segment to the twenty-five institutions receiving the greatest number of test-score submissions from that segment. In 1980 the Higher Education Finance Research Institute performed a confidential analysis of overlap among COFHE institutions at three levels: test-score submission, admission, matriculation. Not surprisingly, that analysis documented a transitive preference ordering among COFHE institutions at each level. Noting this fact, Larry Litten has cautioned that our analysis of CUEPP data may, in fact, overstate the level of competition among some institutions, particularly when large numbers of prospective students consistently preferred one institution over another. In such cases there is not a truly reciprocal relationship between the students' first choice and their "safety" school.

7. In the South, denominational colleges often play similar roles. Given their smaller size, however, these colleges cannot be said to help "structure competition" as do their Catholic counterparts in New England and the Middle States.

8. Our structural analyses occasionally encounter a problem of scale. A university may loom large as a competitor for a small college without the reverse being true. Because we have insisted that competitive relationships be reciprocal, these one-way competitions are not indicated on the schematics.

9. The computer program that performed these analyses processed a maximum of fifty institutions per market segment. Subsequent analysis demonstrated that the fifty most often named institutions accounted for upward of 95 percent of all activity in each segment. Data are printed only for those segments in which the sample institution was ranked among the top fifty institutions.

10. Because there are fewer private flagships in the South, their aggregate role in structuring the region's competition is less pronounced than in New England.

11. These overlap analyses differ from the Tinker Toy analyses presented earlier in two important ways. First, all overlaps were included, not just those 15-percent reciprocal overlaps. Second, the overlap analyses include the fifty, rather than the twenty-five, most often named institutions in each market segment.

12. In the following analyses (Tables 4.7 and 4.8 and Figures 4.6 and 4.7) we exclude local students, since their choice sets are circumscribed by the particular mix of institutions available to them in their own market. We have also limited the analyses to four-year institutions, for which our data are most complete.

13. Because New England has only four linking institutions, the opportunities for overlap with this institutional type are restricted.

14. See Chapter 3, pp. 30–33.

5

Tomorrow's Dilemma: Pools, Prices, and Policies

On many campuses, fall is the time of the president's lament, when collegiate leaders make an effort to inform and warn their communities about the likely consequences of impending enrollment declines. Relying primarily on broad-gauged enrollment projections, the president paints a sobering picture of higher education's future. Not only will many colleges and universities be lacking students in sufficient number to preserve educational quality, but the cultural and scientific resources higher education provides to society at large will be threatened by a kind of intellectual hardening of the arteries, as fewer scholars of real talent are attracted to academic pursuits. In this environment, every college must prepare itself for the possibility that reductions in institutional scale will prove necessary to preserve educational integrity as well as financial viability.

Come spring, however, and the submission of the annual budget, presidential focus and rhetoric change. Gone is the concentration on long-term enrollment declines. Indeed, more often than not, the budget is predicated on a small but sustaining increase in enrollment, despite last fall's exhortations on the need for eventual reductions in institutional scale. What concerns the president in the spring are the immediate problems of a diminishing resource base. Now the president's lament details inflation's continued tax on the economic status of the faculty and staff, the further deterioration of the physical plant, and the inability to make critical investments in new fields of knowledge. When asked why they do not attempt to consolidate their institutions in anticipation of long-term enrollment declines, many presidents respond by belittling the projections they so convincingly cited in the fall. No one, they point out, can be sure that the rate of college participation will not increase; in any case, the projections themselves often vary.

This attitude should not be dismissed as just one more example of higher education's ability to deny the magnitude of its own problems. In fact, what these college presidents are expressing is the conviction that their institutions' very survival depends on enrollment growth. Given the current economic climate, most colleges cannot hope to reduce their reliance on tuition income by cultivating alternative sources of revenue, and inflation limits the effectiveness of cost cutting. Two basic options remain: institutional consolidation or enrollment expansion. As a means to achieve financial viability, institutional contraction offers compelling advantages; as a transformation, or violation, of the educational community, it carries serious risks. Thus, most collegiate leaders seek instead to increase their institutions' shares of a declining student market, allowing the question of scale to recede into an abstract, seemingly distant future. The result is a kind of campus boosterism that maintains, "We are simply going to work harder and buck the trend." Everywhere faculty, students, staff, administrators, and trustees are encouraged to try harder, work longer hours, spend less money, and still enhance the institution's appeal to a restless and diminishing clientele.

Much of this energy will prove purposeful. Over the next decade, admissions officers will add to their folklore hundreds of stories detailing how struggling institutions pulled themselves up by their bootstraps, reaching out to new markets, imaginatively packaging their educational offerings, and welcoming busloads of students who in earlier times would not have even considered applying. Since it is the admissions officers' folklore, there will be less emphasis on the achievement of economic efficiencies or the adoption of new instructional technologies, although these will play a role. Most institutions will thrive or fail on their own energies and cleverness as well as by drawing on their traditional strengths and constituencies.

Yet inevitably failures will loom as large as successes, and the failures, too, will find their way into the admissions officers' lore. There will be a spate of stories of failed advertising campaigns, of extravagant promises the offending institution could not keep, of demoralized faculty, departing students, deteriorating buildings, and finally, of institutional closings.[1] By the end of this decade, there most assuredly will be fewer institutions of higher education than there are today.

Clearly, no institution will quietly close its doors simply because our, or any other, analysis suggests bleak enrollment prospects. Indeed, every college has a special obligation to take whatever steps it judges necessary to strengthen its institutional viability and preserve its educational mission. The current success of Wilson College, though its future is not yet secure, testifies to the wisdom of the court's mandate that the college try again.[2] Still, our data can help an institution calibrate the risks of the 1980s, suggesting the level of effort required to sustain enrollment on the one hand and some possible parameters for institutional consolidation on the other. As observers of, and participants in, this transition for higher education, public policy makers can use the same data to guide their involvement in monitoring educational quality and fostering institutional cooperation.

In order to evaluate the likely distribution of college-bound students among different types of colleges and universities over the coming decade, we first must understand the forces that will shape aggregate demand for higher education. Two basic factors determine the demand for higher education: population (the number of students graduating from high school) and participation rate (the proportion of students who enroll in post-secondary institutions, either immediately following their high school graduation or later). What has fueled the growth in college enrollments over the last 30 years, for example, is both a substantial increase in the number of high school graduates and, until recently, increases in the rate at which these students participated in post-secondary education. As a result, first-time college enrollments grew from 512,000 in 1950 to 1,299,000 in 1979.[3]

While the number of high school graduates for any given year is relatively fixed, the rate of college participation is sensitive to a number of factors. Government policies, social constraints, and economic trends all have played a role in the rising participation rates of the last 30 years. For the nation's minorities and for most of its low-income groups, the gradual reduction of social and economic barriers to a higher education has caused a major increase in participation rates. The same trend has been true for women; the college participation rate for females in most regions of the country now matches or exceeds that for males.

Significantly, the participation rate for males has decreased in recent years: peaking at 35.4 percent in 1975, the rate had dropped to 31.9 percent by 1979. In part, this decline may be attributed to the termination of draft deferments in 1972, but it also may reflect a reduction in the extra earnings expected by college graduates. Generally speaking, the rate of college participation increases when the rate of return on investment (college costs plus foregone earnings) rises in terms of increased lifelong earnings. The participation rate, in other words, increases whenever the best way to "get ahead" is to get a college education. In the growing economy of the 1950s and 1960s, college students had the opportunity to confirm this maxim.[4]

In the 1970s, another major force buoyed college participation rates, as the federal government set out to ensure that no student in America was denied a college or university education for want of financial resources. Once enacted by Congress, new federal programs—Pell Grants, Supplemental Education Opportunity Grants, College Work Study, NDSLs, GSLs, HEALS, ALAS—transformed the federal government into the dominant "third-party payer" for higher education in the same way that Medicare, Medicaid, Blue Cross, Blue Shield, and private insurance plans had become the health industry's third-party payers. Jobs and direct grants were made available to economically disadvantaged students, and most other students were recipients of federal loans. In this way, it became possible for students to choose among a broad range of institutions—private or public, expensive or inexpensive, selective or open-door. Today it is not at all uncommon, even at private, highly selective institutions, for two-thirds of the student body to be direct beneficiaries of federal programs of financial assistance.[5]

On the question of future trends in college participation rates, the jury is still out. Since 1975 the overall rate has flattened, despite fluctuations in the rates for different groups. Much could depend on the relationship between demographic and economic patterns. Whenever there is a rapid increase in the size of the 18- to 24-year-old cohort, the economy simply cannot create enough new jobs to accommodate all of the nation's youth. The last half of the 1970s, when individuals born during the peak of the baby boom reached college and work age, represents a classic example of the effect that cohort crowding can have on both the economy and the college participation rate. For a while, college enrollments increased because the young people had nowhere else to go. Over the long run, however, the economic value of their education diminished precisely because the supply of college-educated workers outpaced the economy's demand. This overcrowding, however, began to ease in 1980, when the number of young people started to decline. Some observers, including Richard Easterlin and his colleagues, view this as a promising development, arguing that college participation rates should now continue their natural rise as a recovering economy seeks new college-educated workers.[6]

If the likely direction of college participation rates in the 1980s remains unknown, the level of decline in the number of high school graduates is clear. In 1980, public and private secondary schools across New England, for example, graduated just under 190,000 students. Michael Tierney now estimates that by 1985, New England secondary schools will graduate 16.5 percent fewer students, for a total of 159,000. Tierney's projection results from a school district by school district analysis of students currently in grades seven through twelve and from a weighted three-year average reflecting their persistence to graduation. Based on actual enrollments and current rates of attrition within individual school systems, these estimates take account of migration patterns.[7]

Assuming for the moment that college participation rates remain constant for the next few years, how will the decline in population affect aggregate demand for higher education? We know that slightly more than 120,000 of the region's 190,000 graduating high school seniors took the SAT examination in 1980 and that about 96,000 submitted their scores to at least one college or university or to an accredited technical, vo-technical, or allied health program. On the basis of this information, we can estimate that the 1980 college participation rate for high school seniors going directly to a post-secondary institution ranged somewhere between 50 and 63 percent, a finding consistent with Tierney's analysis of the college participation rate as reflected in the Bureau of the Census' *Current Population Survey* (CPS).[8] In this way, we can project aggregate demand as follows: if by 1985 the population of high school graduates declines by 31,000 students as compared to 1980, and if the estimated 1980 college participation rate of 50–63 percent remains constant, then in 1985 between 16,000 and 38,000 fewer first-year students will enroll in New England's post-secondary institutions than enrolled five years earlier. Among the six states of the region, there would be a range of enrollment shifts. While no state would actually increase its number of high school graduates, New Hampshire's loss would be less than 10 percent, while the other two northern states, Maine and Vermont, would also experience below-average declines—11.5 and 15.0 percent, respectively. The three southern New England states would all experience above-average declines: Massachusetts, 17.1 percent; Connecticut, 18.6 percent; and Rhode Island, 20.3 percent.[9]

These numbers still do not tell us about the enrollment prospects of individual colleges and universities. That there will be fewer students is hardly news; what college presidents, faculties, and trustees want to know is, "Will our institution be one of those that are forced to contract or even close?" To assess the likely distribution of students among different types of institutions under the conditions outlined above, we

Figure 5.1. Uniform-Draw Model of College Applicants

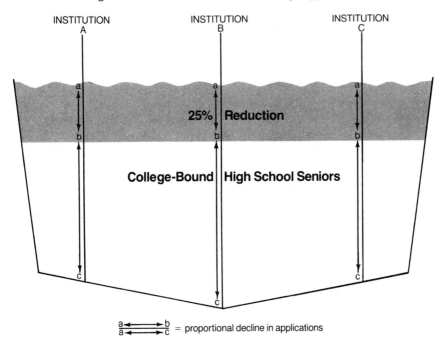

$\dfrac{a}{a} \longleftrightarrow \dfrac{b}{c}$ = proportional decline in applications

need once again to visualize the structure of institutional competition. Discussions of student demographics and distribution usually revolve around two general, if oversimplified, notions of how a declining pool of students affects individual institutions. The argument between the two positions reduces itself to a question of relative risk. When the supply of potential college students declines, will all institutions be affected proportionally, or will some institutions be affected very little while others are forced to close for lack of clientele?

It is probably easiest to understand these two positions by making explicit the pool metaphor each uses when describing the supply of students. Imagine, in the first instance, a pool of water with reasonably steep sides and a relatively flat bottom (Figure 5.1). Institutions can be located in almost any place in the pool and still have a relatively uniform draw. When such a pool loses 25 percent of its contents, each of the institutions, irrespective of its place in the pool, will lose roughly 25 percent of its applicants. Only those institutions at the very margin are likely to have their shares of the pool evaporate entirely.

The counter argument pictures a pool with a deep center and sloping sides (Figure 5.2). In such a pool, it matters a great deal whether the institution is at the center or periphery; for as this pool shrinks by 25 percent, institutions at its center will hardly be affected. Those not safely in the center of the pool, however, can expect dramatic reductions in their shares of the pool's contents. Proponents of this viewpoint explain such a configuration of the student pool by pointing to the traditional pecking order among institutions. On the one hand, the most selective institutions need to become only a little less selective to maintain their overall size. Institutions already practicing open admissions, on the other hand, will be able to maintain their size only by drastically reducing their prices in order to retain the necessary volume of students.

In fact, neither image of the student pool captures our understanding of the structure of college choice. The appearance of but a single surface to the pool hides the fact that, in reality, there are series of linked basins carved out of the pool's uneven bottom (Figure 5.3). At one end is a steep-sided, deep basin of students who have traditionally applied to selective, high-cost private institutions. At the center of this basin, there is security, for here lie institutions that currently admit less than a third of the students who apply and matriculate more than half of those admitted. At the basin's edge, however, we find selective institutions that already admit more than half of the students who apply and matriculate less than a third of those they admit. These institutions are at risk despite their traditional aura of success and invincibility.

Figure 5.2. Simple-Hierarchy Model of College Applicants

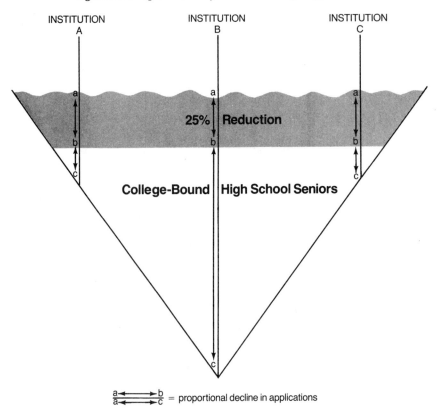

Figure 5.3. Linked-Basins Model of College Applicants

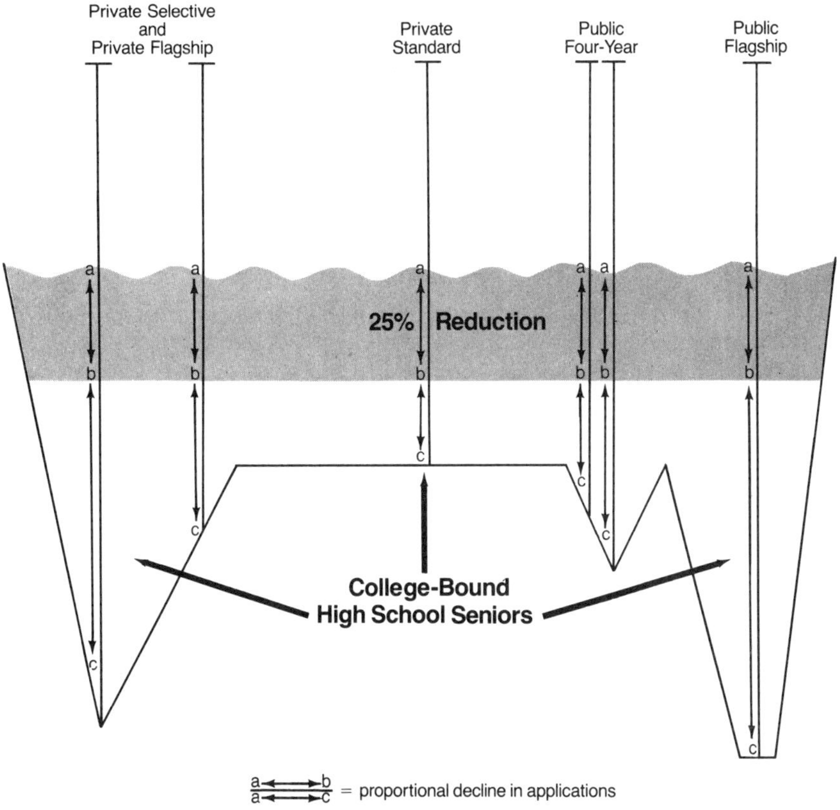

Private Selective
and
Private Flagship

Private
Standard

Public
Four-Year

Public
Flagship

25% Reduction

College-Bound
High School Seniors

$$\frac{a \leftarrow\!\!\rightarrow b}{a \leftarrow\!\!\rightarrow c} = \text{proportional decline in applications}$$

There is a second deep basin from which the public flagships draw most of their students and an adjoining basin from which the state colleges and, on occasion, community colleges draw their students. Between these deeper basins is an area of shallows that supplies most private standard colleges with students. Connected both to the high-ability/high-cost basin and the public basins, this broad middle section of the pool contains roughly half of all college-bound students in New England, though only when the other basins are full. Once the pool begins to lose volume, those institutions centered in this broadly private sector of the market will be the most exposed.

The concept of distinct though adjoining student basins corresponding to different institutional types is simply a recasting of the competitive overlap principle embodied in our Tinker Toy diagrams (see Chapter 4). By and large, institutions of a given type compete with one another for a particular set of students. Though there is some flow of students between institutional types within a given sector (public or private), the highly ordered socioeconomic structure of student choice dampens such competition. Even less frequent is competition across sectors, between public and private institutions. Thus, it is the depth of the specific basin from which a given institution draws its students that will largely determine its enrollment potential, not the institution's status vis-à-vis institutions of a different type.[10]

The perceived depth of a given basin, however, depends on one's position within it. For this reason, the individual college or university must determine its standing in relation to other institutions of the same type. Since every institutional type has this internal hierarchy, it follows that the less-selective institutions within every type will feel the effects of a dwindling population of college-bound students; but entire sets of institutions will become vulnerable only insofar as their pools already are shallow, as in the case of private standard colleges. We may, in other words, witness a number of institutional closings in the 1980s, but no single type of institution will become extinct.

The factors that hold competition largely within the boundaries of a given institutional type are resistant, but not immune, to external social and economic pressures. Still assuming constant college participation rates and a reasonably stable economy, the reduction in demand for higher education caused by the end of the baby boom could produce some limited exceptions to the general rule of like competing with like. Though we envision no mass migration from private to public institutions, each sector may well experience a shift from one institutional type to another as college-bound students take advantage of the excess capacity of the more-selective groups of institutions. In the private sector, the nonselective institutions could begin losing students to the selective private colleges and universities; a similar rationale of "shopping up" could apply in the public sector, with students abandoning the state colleges in favor of the more prestigious public flagships.

Thus far we have been exploring the distributional consequences of reductions in the number of high school graduates. Demographic shifts, however, constitute only half of the equation defining demand for higher education. What if participation, as well as population, diminishes in the years ahead? In the early stages of the debate over the effect of impending population declines, Stephen Dresch predicted a 40-percent decrease in college enrollments during the 1980s. Looking at the same demographic fact that underlay Easterlin's prediction of increased college participation rates—the replacement of a large cohort of youth by a much smaller cohort—Dresch arrived at an opposite conclusion. When the baby boom ended, Dresch argued, not only would there be fewer high school seniors to populate the nation's colleges, but there would be fewer high school seniors to fill new jobs in the economy. In fact, the oversupply of first-time workers in the 1970s would give way to an equally significant undersupply, forcing each sector of the economy to increase wages in order to attract enough new workers. As wages increased, so would the foregone earnings of those attending college, causing the net return of a college education to decrease. Over the long run, Dresch concluded, we would witness a significantly lower college participation rate for the 18- to 24-year-old age cohort. One did not need to accept the economic modeling that guided Dresch's analysis to understand that a growing economy in the 1980s could lead to open competition for young people between industry and the nation's colleges and universities.[11]

In recent years, Dresch's projections have lost their edge in many circles. Though 1980 officially marked the end of the baby boom, college enrollments overall did not falter, suggesting that population declines were being offset by increases, rather than decreases, in the rate of college participation. Nor have observers seen signs of industry "stealing" students. Indeed, the nation's sluggish economy requires fewer rather than more employees, and new technologies may reduce, rather than increase, the need for additional first-time workers.[12]

Our ability to undercut Dresch's arguments should not lull us into a false sense of security regarding the likely direction of college participation rates. Ironically, in the long run Dresch's aggregate enrollment projections could prove right, though for all the wrong reasons. During a recession, college enrollments tend to rise as unemployment increases among college-age youth. When work is scarce, foregone

earnings decline, and the likelihood of individual young people enrolling in college increases, if only temporarily. Eventually, however,
persistent economic stagnation and underemployment decrease college
enrollments by reducing the number of good jobs for new graduates.
Today, the observed delays in expected enrollment declines could represent the calm before the storm rather than a natural and continuing
rise in college participation as Easterlin would suggest. Increasingly,
economists have begun to talk about a long-term slide in the economy's
ability to generate substantial growth. The prospect is for a decade or
more in which individuals, as well as institutions, will be hard pressed
to realize their ambitions.[13]

This worst-case scenario has serious implications for higher education in general and college enrollments in particular. Sluggish economic growth and continued underemployment would further deflate
the college participation rate. The need to reduce federal expenditures
in order to bring expense more in line with income would likely lead to
reductions not only in student financial assistance but also in that
broad range of federal programs that provide institutions of higher
education with critical funds to invest in new research, programs, and
facilities. Finally, a sluggish economy would have the same chilling
effect on state and local governments, leading them to cap and, whenever possible, reduce appropriations for higher education. Declines in
the number of high school graduates would provide all the rationale a
hard-pressed governor or state legislature required to keep per-student
cost constant, thereby lowering the total appropriations to higher
education.

To summarize our assumptions under this worst-case scenario: if the
nation is entering a long and sustained period of economic uncertainty,
then we can expect a substantial decrease in the demand for higher
education occasioned in part by the end of the baby boom, in part by
a lessening of the economic returns attached to a college education, and
in part by a general decline in public subsidies to both students and
institutions. Under these conditions, individual colleges and universities obviously would be subject to further declines in enrollment. To
what extent, however, could we expect the distribution of students
among competing institutions to change? As we have seen, our analysis of population declines alone suggests only limited competition
across institutional types and no major violation of the boundary between public and private institutions. Could the current structure of
college choice endure the additional stress of substantial declines in
the participation rate?

Many observers argue that the first consequence of this worst-case scenario would be a pronounced shift in enrollments from private to public institutions. High-ability students, in particular, would switch their allegiance to public institutions in order to reserve their own and their families' savings for the increasingly costly courses of graduate and professional education to which they also aspire. We cannot be sure that such a mass migration would not take place, but the social and economic logic of college choice clearly militates against it. The very economic forces that might drive students toward the public sector would also make public institutions more costly or less desirable to these students. The same declining revenues and soaring deficits that would compel the federal government to limit financial assistance to individual students would similarly oblige state legislatures and city or county agencies to reduce their direct appropriations to public institutions of higher education. Whether it were a Proposition 13 or a Proposition 2½ that captured the voters' fancy, there would be a growing belief that as the number of high school graduates declined, so should the state's bill for higher education.

Under these conditions, three general strategies would be available to public institutions: they could increase tuition to offset the loss of public appropriations, limit enrollments in order to limit their costs, or decrease the average amount spent on each student.[14] The result of the first option obviously would be to lessen the price differential between public and private sectors, thus reducing the likely net flow of students from private to public institutions. In the second case, the limiting of enrollments to match resources would create a rationing mechanism that would necessarily retard the flow of students from private to public institutions. If public institutions, in the third instance, maintained enrollments despite decreased appropriations, the price differential between public and private education would be retained, but the necessary overcrowding of public institutions would make them significantly less attractive to students who in the past had sought private options.

In this way, the traditional structure of college choice is likely to absorb all but the most drastic of economic shocks. Under both of our scenarios—population declines alone or population declines compounded by diminishing participation and a lagging economy—we foresee a basic continuation of the current separation between the public and private sectors. Within each sector, however, increased competition between formerly distinct institutional types is likely to occur. Our first scenario—declining population, constant participation, stable economy—posited two such shifts. Students who in earlier years would have been limited to nonselective private colleges might qualify for the more-selective private institutions, while students in the state colleges pool turned their attention to the public flagships.

Under our worst-case scenario, however, most students would no longer have the luxury of shopping up. Differences in price between institutional types (within the same sector) could lead, in this instance, to significant changes in the structure of competition. Some of the major casualties could prove to be a few of the nation's better-known private research universities that have come to depend too heavily on undergraduate enrollments to finance their general operations. The irony is that the threat would come not from increased competition with the public sector, but from competition with other private institutions. In New England just fifty-six institutions provide principal competition in the high-ability/high-cost student market—twenty-one major research universities and thirty-five selective four-year colleges.[15] From the student's viewpoint, what distinguishes the two types are differences in scale and setting. Private flagships are large, complex, frequently urban (and sometimes impersonal) institutions whose strength lies in the range of their academic offerings and experiences. Selective colleges, on the other hand, are smaller, often rural institutions offering a more-concentrated curriculum and promising the kind of personalized education only possible on a relatively small campus principally devoted to undergraduate life. There is, however, no essential difference in the price between a private flagship university and a private selective college. Not wholly by coincidence, tuition, room, and board charges at the two types of institutions fall within a remarkably narrow range, and frequently the financial aid offers they make to individual students are identical. In the high-ability/high-cost student market, price currently plays no role simply because it varies so little.

We suspect that this price parity would not be maintained during a decade of persistent economic distress. Rather, growing price competition between private flagships and private selective colleges would become an increasingly unpleasant fact of life. Private research universities inherently face more severe economic problems than private selective colleges do. In the 1970s these universities maintained their quality largely by increasing their tuition incomes fast enough to offset inflation's tax on their other principal sources of income: endowment, gifts, and sponsored research. Most private flagships in the 1970s increased not only the price of their undergraduate programs but their scale, so that by the end of the decade tuition income from undergraduate education was often the largest single source of unrestricted funds available to the institution. The 1980s could promise more of the same, obliging most private flagships to choose between increasing tuition faster than inflation or actually increasing the size of their student bodies, despite sharp decreases in the overall demand for higher education.

Private selective colleges would not face a similar dilemma primarily because these institutions, provided they were able to maintain enrollment, could settle for increases in the tuition rate that matched general increases in the cost of goods and services. Put simply, private selective colleges would not require the same tuition rate increases that the private flagships would require if they were unable to increase enrollment. Recall that seven of every ten students interested in a private flagship in 1980 were also interested in a private selective college (see Table 4.8). As the competition for these students continues to intensify — as each institution competing in the high-ability/high-cost market seeks to sustain or expand its enrollment — the temptation for private selective colleges to differentiate themselves from private flagships on the basis of price could prove irresistible. The other possibility is that some private selective colleges would choose to maintain price parity with the private flagships but would use the extra funds to increase their financial aid budgets — simply a more subtle form of price competition.[16]

At the same time, there could be a genuine winnowing of both types of institutions now competing in the high-ability/high-cost student market. A kind of aura surrounds institutions that compete successfully in this market, a belief that they choose their students as much as their students choose them. A 30- to 40-percent decline in the demand for higher education would mean, if nothing else, dramatically fewer students for the selective private institutions to turn down. Even today some selective colleges are having to dig deeply into their applicant pools in order to satisfy their enrollment needs. As the demand for higher education decreases over the next decade, a significant number of these institutions could slip from being selective colleges to become, in our terms, private standard colleges. While this process would be traumatic for colleges forced to endure a seemingly irrational devaluing of their product, these institutions would still be in a better position than the private flagship no longer able to enroll enough new freshmen to preserve its internal economy.

It is, however, within that broad category of private standard colleges that the greatest effects of a precipitous drop in college enrollments would be felt. Competing predominantly for in-state students, these institutions face stiff public competition even when times are good. Under a worst-case scenario, they would be hard pressed to sustain their enrollments. Some would fail, their prospective students

taken by more-selective private colleges (as in our first scenario) or by
public institutions providing a less costly educational alternative. How
many of the 187 nonselective private institutions that in 1980 competed
for students would close would depend on both the actual decline in
the demand for higher education and changes in the cost of providing
education.

The public sector, too, would be subject to internal migrations
across institutional types. Public flagships, because of their marginally
greater expense than public four-year institutions, would likely lose
some enrollments to state colleges, particularly if economic conditions
forced a significant number of students to switch from residential to
commuting status. Public flagships in remote areas without a natural
commuter pool upon which to draw could experience major declines in
their enrollments if hard times persisted throughout the decade. State
colleges, on the other hand, would be as likely to lose students to community colleges as they would be to gain enrollments from the public
flagship. Finally, community colleges, the traditional port of entry to
the educational system for students most affected by marginal changes
in the college participation rate, would likely see their gains offset by
losses among students who were entirely driven out of the educational
market by bad times.[17]

In summary, even a 30-percent or more decline in the demand for
higher education should not significantly weaken the barrier between
public and private competition. The very conditions that might propel
students from the private to the public sector would also result in
higher tuitions for public education or readily apparent declines in the
quality of public higher education. Nonetheless, all students would
tend to become more price-conscious educational consumers, laying
the groundwork for dramatically increased price competition across
institutional types within each sector of the college market.

Thus, while both scenarios show the largely separate character of
public and private competition, the worst-case analysis exhibits more
shifts in competition between institutional types. In the case of population declines alone, such shifts are seen to occur in only two cases, as
students turn from private standard colleges to more-selective private
institutions and from state colleges to public flagships. When population declines are compounded by falling participation rates and economic distress, some shifting can be expected on every level. Even institutional types likely to increase their share of the market could face
a decade of diminished demand. Private selective colleges, for example,
could draw prestige-conscious students from private standard colleges
but still find their enrollment levels and perceived quality in jeopardy.

The big losers in the private sector, however, would come from two very different institutional types. First, a few major research universities could fail to fill their undergraduate classes without significantly reducing their prices and thus undermining their internal economies. Second, a number of private standard colleges could be put out of business when their traditional student pools were diverted either to private selective colleges or low-cost public institutions. Changes in the public sector would be more straightforward, as students seeking to minimize educational costs began to switch from public flagships to state colleges and from state colleges to community colleges. Such changes could also be accompanied by an increase in the number of students deciding to live at home and commute.

Given these patterns of institutional competition, there is much that can be said for a public policy that lets the market work its will in the coming decade. To some extent, the ominous overtones of such an assertion are unavoidable: whether enrollment declines are closer to 15 percent or 30 percent, we are certain to witness some disturbing consequences as individual institutions fight for their survival. If the nation does, in fact, face a decade of economic stagnation and unemployment on the one hand and declining public support for higher education on the other, the consequences obviously will be more severe. Money does matter, and its absence, coupled with the declining demand for higher education, inevitably will kindle intense competition for students at every juncture. Still, the basic diversity of the nation's system of higher education does not appear to be in jeopardy. Institutions of all types will be affected by diminishing pools and increased competition, but no single type will disappear; nor will the public sector put the private sector out of business.

Even if public policy makers did attempt to control the fates of different types of institutions, there is little evidence that such intervention could be accomplished successfully, particularly in view of declining public appropriations for higher education. In theory, state legislatures could reduce appropriations selectively, shifting monies, for example, from programs of student aid to direct appropriations for publicly owned colleges and universities. Or legislatures could accept the closing of marginal public campuses and use the resulting monies to invest in targeted institutions, thus improving the quality of academic programs within the state. In practice, however, the log-rolling nature of the political process almost guarantees that reductions in higher education appropriations will be shared proportionately by all programs. In pursuit of fairness, legislatures will expect each element of the higher education system to share the pain of budget cuts. If these proportional reductions are accompanied by an insistence that no public campus be closed, then the economic leverage available to state policy makers will prove illusory.

Most state agencies have already learned that their power to regulate competition for students is limited. Program proliferation among academic institutions has become a way of life. Even within state college systems, there are few examples of successful program coordination or control. While some state departments of education may speak of their ability to ration students, either across the public and private sectors or within the public sector, we frankly doubt they have such power. We are also skeptical of attempts to secure the voluntary limiting of enrollments by individual institutions. No institution is prepared to share enrollments or to abandon some programs on the promise that its competitors will relinquish others. The problem is that no single institution, or even set of institutions, controls enough of the market to establish a cartel capable of managing the distribution of enrollments among its members. As Fred Crossland is so fond of pointing out, higher education remains a cottage industry. Even the most prestigious and well-endowed university serves less than 5 percent of its potential market. It is a cottage industry, moreover, in which the most intense competition is among remarkably similar institutions.

Our own conclusion is that the market mechanism ought to be allowed to control the distribution of students among competing institutions, provided that some institutions are not given unfair advantage and that basic standards of educational quality are maintained. In this context, public policy could play a constructive role by encouraging institutional autonomy, monitoring academic standards, and promoting interinstitutional cooperation. In sum, we urge public policy makers to consider three basic recommendations.

- First, if public appropriations to state-owned institutions are to be reduced, those institutions should have the right to set their own tuitions and to retain their tuition income. To limit expenditures without limiting enrollment or allowing tuitions to seek a natural market level will lead inexorably to a devaluing of public higher education that could surpass today's general devaluing of public primary and secondary education.
- Second, state agencies should invest their attention, energies, and political leverage in strengthening their state's system of academic accreditation. Only public agencies, in the final analysis, have the power to insist that institutions cannot preserve enrollments by changing the nature of their educational degrees.

▪ Third, public agencies that seek to foster voluntary cooperation among institutions should focus not on the sharing of enrollments but on the sharing of facilities. Most institutions would be able to survive the initial shock of enrollment declines if they could reduce their space-related costs by 15 percent or more. These efficiencies will prove possible only if separate colleges and universities learn to share campuses, laboratories, and even scarce faculty. In time, perhaps, genuine enrollment sharing and program integration could grow out of these efforts. For the moment, however, public programs with real incentives for facility sharing among colleges and universities should become a first priority of public policy.

Ultimately, it is the institutions themselves, not the state, that must be responsible for preventing the worst of the market horrors envisioned for the 1980s. Each spring, it is the obligation of every college president to recall what he or she said in the fall. If, after due consideration, the judgment still is to try harder rather than to retrench, then at least the institution should try harder within the most purposeful and rational framework available — recruiting students from communities with a demonstrated predisposition toward the type of education offered and cultivating opportunities for communication and cooperation with other institutions. If even the most reasoned and energetic efforts cannot bolster sagging enrollments, then deliberate consolidation should be the next step.

In the final analysis, institutional viability must depend more on quality than quantity — the perceived value of the educational process rather than the volume of students engaged in that process. For this reason, institutional scale should be derived rather than predetermined, with educational quality acting as the independent variable. The difficulty, during times of diminishing student demand, lies in reducing the high fixed costs associated with personnel commitments and physical plant. Colleges and universities simply do not have the kind of part-time staff and convertible space that would allow them to gear production to demand. Indeed, one parody portrays academe as a monastery seeking first to maximize its number of monks and only secondarily to employ them productively.[18] In truth, all good colleges and universities endlessly seek to expand their educational resources, to extend the boundaries of new knowledge. Yet intellectual chemistry is created by the interaction among teachers, students, and environment; and a critical balance must be maintained during periods of contraction as well as growth. In the years ahead, higher education should perhaps devote as much attention to analyzing fixed costs as to planning recruiting strategies. By working together as well as separately, colleges and universities should be able to develop new approaches not only to issues of facilities and personnel management but also to the problem of student financial assistance.

We believe that the system of higher education that emerges at the end of this decade can be stronger, more efficient, more prepared to invest in new ideas and technologies. We understand, though, that the converse may prove true. More than a decade of intense competition, coupled with severe underfunding, could permanently devalue the nation's colleges and universities. It is a question of purposefulness as well as result. We began our study in search of an understanding of college enrollments that would allow institutions to gauge their own futures in terms of the likely scale of their educational offerings. We end with a hope that most colleges and universities will grow stronger precisely because they will become more efficient in the management of resources even as they become more resourceful in their search for new students.

Notes

1. See, for example, Edward B. Fiske, "The Marketing of the Colleges," *Atlantic Monthly* (October 1979) pp. 93–98.

2. *Wilson College: A Case Study,* (Indianapolis: Lily Endowment, Inc., 1979).

3. Michael Tierney, *Trends in College Participation Rates,* (Boulder: National Center for Higher Education Management Systems, 1982); Humphrey Doerman, *Toward Equal Access,* (New York: The College Board, 1978).

4. Tierney, *Trends in College Participation Rates,* p. 32. It is important to note that the rate at which high school graduates go on to college is considerably higher than the college participation rate for 18 to 21 year olds, a group that includes students who did not graduate from high school. On the economic returns of a college education see, for example, Lewis C. Solomon and Paul J. Taubman, eds., *Does College Matter?* (New York: Academic Press, 1973).

5. College Scholarship Service, *Meeting College Costs,* annual publication.

6. Dennis Ahlburg, Eileen M. Crimmuns, Richard A. Easterlin, "The Outlook for Higher Education: A Cohort Size Model of Enrollment of the College Age Population, 1948–2000," *Review of Public Data Use* (1981) 9:211–227; Michael Wachter, "Economic Challenges Posed by Demographic Changes," in Eli Ginsberg et al., *Work Decisions in the 1980s,* (Boston: Auburn House, 1982).

7. Professor Tierney's estimates are supplied as a regular CUEPP service in "High School Graduates by Market."

8. Tierney, *Trends in College Participation Rates.*

9. Estimates for the five Southern States are: Virginia, −5.7 percent; North Carolina, 10.1 percent; South Carolina, 2.5 percent; Georgia, −6.9 percent; and Florida, 0.4 percent.

10. For the purposes of the pool metaphor, we have combined private flagships with private selective institutions, since these two types (unlike the others) do exhibit a high degree of overlap.

11. Stephen Dresch, "Demography, Technology, and Higher Education: Towards a Formal Model of Education Adaptation," *Journal of Political Economy* (1975) 83:535–569.

12. This conclusion is based in part on the Higher Education Finance Research Institute's study of corporate training and education, Martin Meyerson and Robert Zemsky principal investigators.

13. See, for example, Michael L. Wachter and Susan M. Wachter, eds., *Toward a New U.S. Industrial Policy*, (Philadelphia: University of Pennsylvania Press, 1983).

14. We are aware of public discussion of these alternatives in Pennsylvania, Connecticut, and California.

15. See Table 4.7, p. 66.

16. In large part, this analysis reflects the experience of COFHE institutions over the last decade.

17. See Humphrey Doerman, *Toward Equal Access*. Doerman analyzes how college participation rates would be affected by increases in federal aid to low-income students. Our analysis asks the opposite question: Would reductions in federal aid similarly decrease participation rates among those most likely to attend a community college?

18. See, in particular, Howard Bowen, *The Costs of Higher Education*, (San Francisco: Jossey-Bass, 1980), for his "revenue theory of expense."

Appendix A: Socioeconomic Attributes in the Middle States and South

Chapter 3 describes in detail the socioeconomic values that appear to structure college choice across New England. These patterns are equally true for students in the Middle States and Southern regions as defined in our study. Paralleling Table 3.4, the data we present below for the two other regions document that a student's market segment (local, in-state, or regional/national) can be explained as an ordered function of the number of basic attributes possessed. Careful readers will note that the ordering is slightly different in each analysis, further illustrating the role of local influences.

Table A.1. Distribution of Middle States Students by Combinations of Attributes

Attributes		Percent*			
Number	Combination	Local	In-State	Regional/ National	Total
0	None	41.6	30.0	28.3	76,052
1	Seeks more than B.A.	35.1	26.6	38.4	39,826
	SATS ≥ 1100	24.9	35.1	39.9	7,510
	Both parents with B.A.	25.0	31.8	43.2	5,896
	Family income ≥ $35,000	25.8	26.1	48.1	12,136
2	More than B.A. + SATS ≥ 1100	18.8	29.9	51.4	11,094
	More than B.A. + Both parents with B.A.	20.4	26.0	53.6	5,393
	More than B.A. + Income ≥ $35,000	18.6	22.1	59.3	7,926
	Both parents with B.A. + SATS ≥ 1100	12.5	26.6	60.9	1,578
	Income ≥ $35,000 + SATS ≥ 1100	12.7	23.8	63.6	1,959
	Income ≥ $35,000 + Both parents with B.A.	14.6	23.6	61.8	5,031
3	More than B.A. + Both parents with B.A. + SATS ≥ 1100	9.0	23.7	67.3	3,690
	More than B.A. + Income ≥ $35,000 + SATS ≥ 1100	7.4	18.0	74.6	4,012
	More than B.A. + Income ≥ $35,000 + Both parents with B.A.	9.9	21.5	68.6	5,578
	Income > $35,000 + Both parents with B.A. + SATS ≥ 1100	6.6	16.5	76.9	1,846
4	All	4.2	13.4	82.4	5,527

*For students reporting given combinations of attributes, the percentages refer to the proportion classified as local, in-state, or regional/national.

Table A.2. Distribution of Southern Students by Combinations of Attributes

Attributes			Percent*		
Number	Combination	Local	In-State	Regional/National	Total
0	None	28.5	50.2	21.2	43,342
1	Family income ≥ $35,000	18.7	51.2	30.1	8,026
	Both parents with B.A.	19.1	50.2	30.7	4,121
	Seeks more than B.A.	20.0	49.1	30.9	23,637
	SATS ≥ 1100	16.7	48.1	35.2	2,944
2	Income ≥ $35,000 + Both parents with B.A.	11.5	49.9	38.6	3,343
	More than B.A. + Income ≥ $35,000	12.2	48.5	39.2	5,152
	More than B.A. + Both parents with B.A.	12.7	44.8	42.6	3,630
	Income ≥ $35,000 + SATS ≥ 1100	10.4	40.0	49.6	935
	Both parents with B.A. + SATS ≥ 1100	8.5	41.0	50.5	730
	More than B.A. + SATS ≥ 1100	10.4	38.3	51.2	4,235
3	More than B.A. + Income ≥ $35,000 + Both parents with B.A.	7.3	42.6	50.1	3,337
	Income ≥ $35,000 + Both parents with B.A. + SATS ≥ 1100	6.3	34.8	58.9	747
	More than B.A. + Income ≥ $35,000 + SATS ≥ 1100	5.8	33.0	61.1	1,800
	More than B.A. + Both parents with B.A. + SATS ≥ 1100	6.5	29.1	64.4	1,818
4	All	2.8	24.3	72.9	2,165

*For students reporting given combinations of attributes, the percentages refer to the proportion classified as local, in-state, or regional/national.

Appendix B1: New England Markets

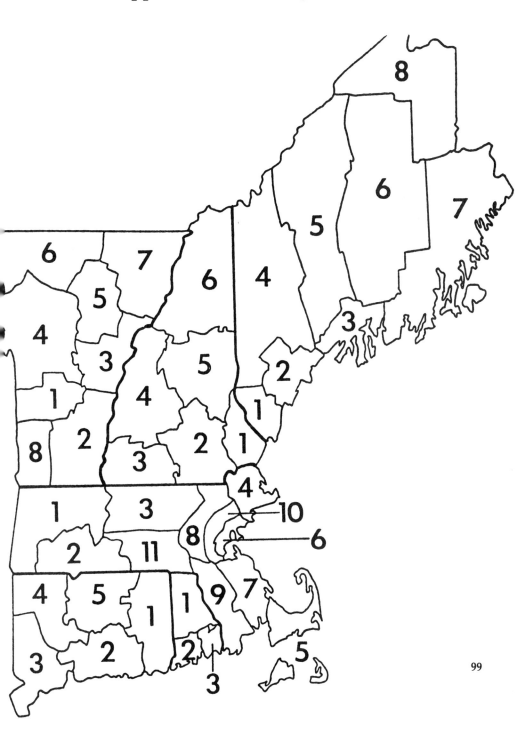

New England Markets

Connecticut
1. New London and Windham County
2. New Haven and Middlesex County
3. Fairfield County
4. Waterbury and Litchfield County
5. Hartford and Tolland County

Maine
1. York County
2. Portland
3. Bath and Rockland
4. Lewiston, Oxford County, and Franklin County
5. Augusta and Somerset County
6. Bangor and Piscataquis County
7. Bar Harbor and Washington County
8. Aroostook County

Massachusetts
1. Berkshire County and Franklin County
2. Springfield and Hampshire County
3. Fitchburg and North Worcester County
4. Essex County
5. Cape Cod and Islands
6. Boston and Cambridge
7. Quincy and Plymouth County
8. Lowell, Concord, and Wellesley
9. Norfolk and Bristol County
10. Malden, Lexington, and Waltham
11. Worcester

New Hampshire
1. Seacoast
2. Merrimack Valley
3. Monadnock
4. Dartmouth and Lake Sunapee
5. Lakes
6. White Mountains

Rhode Island
1. Providence, Warwick, and Woonsocket
2. Kingston and Westerly
3. Newport and Bristol

Vermont
1. Rutland
2. Brattleboro and Windsor
3. Woodstock and Chelsea
4. Burlington and Middlebury
5. Montpelier and Lamoille
6. Franklin County
7. St. Johnsbury, Newport, and Essex County
8. Bennington

Appendix B2: Middle States Markets

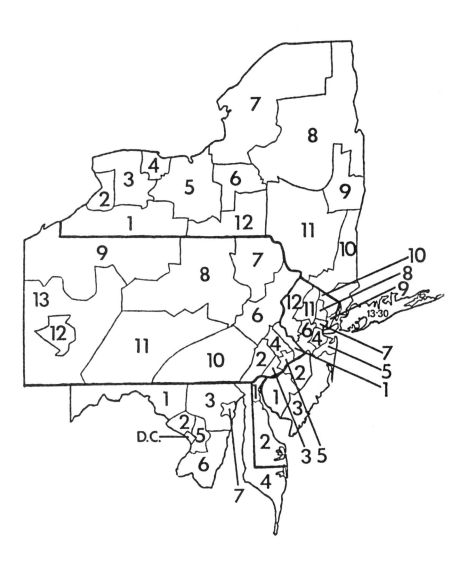

For the greater New York City area (markets 13-30), see detailed map on page 102.

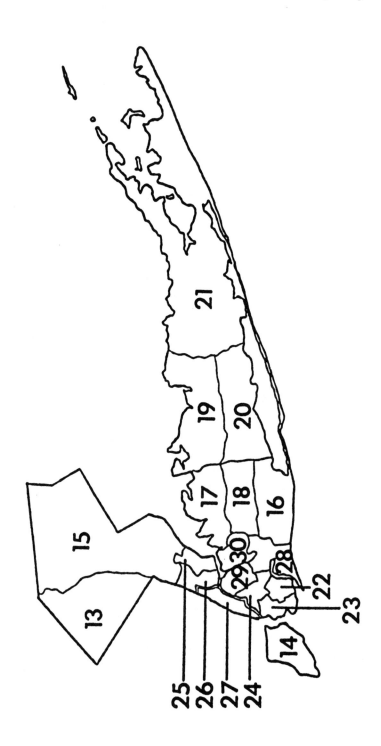

Middle States Markets

Delaware
1. New Castle County
2. Kent County and Sussex County

District of Columbia
1. District of Columbia

Maryland
1. Western Maryland
2. Montgomery Metropolitan
3. Central Maryland without Baltimore
4. Eastern Shore
5. Prince Georges Metropolitan
6. Southern Maryland
7. Baltimore (Urban)

New Jersey
1. Southern Jersey
2. Camden and Burlington County
3. Jersey Shore and Pinelands
4. Middlesex County
5. Monmouth County
6. Somerset County and Mercer County
7. Union County
8. Essex County and Southern Passaic County
9. Hudson County
10. Bergen County
11. Morris County and Northern Passaic County
12. Sussex County, Warren County, and Hunterdon County

New York
1. Southern Tier West
2. Erie County
3. Genessee Valley and Northern Frontier
4. Rochester and Monroe County
5. Finger Lakes Region
6. Central New York
7. St. Lawrence Valley
8. Adirondacks
9. Tri Cities
10. Central Hudson Valley
11. Catskills
12. Southern Tier East
13. Rockland County
14. Staten Island
15. Westchester County
16. Southern Nassau County
17. Northern Nassau County
18. Central Nassau County
19. Northwest Suffolk County
20. Southwest Suffolk County

21. East Suffolk County
22. Southeast Brooklyn
23. West Brooklyn
24. Northeast Brooklyn
25. East Bronx
26. West Bronx
27. Manhattan
28. South Queens
29. Northwest Queens
30. Northeast Queens

Pennsylvania
 1. Bucks County
 2. Chester County
 3. Delaware County
 4. Montgomery County
 5. Philadelphia County
 6. Lehigh Valley
 7. Northeastern Pennsylvania
 8. North Central Pennsylvania
 9. Northwestern Pennsylvania
10. Southern Pennsylvania—East
11. Southern Pennsylvania—West
12. Allegheny County
13. Southwest Pennsylvania without Allegheny County

Appendix B3: Southern Markets

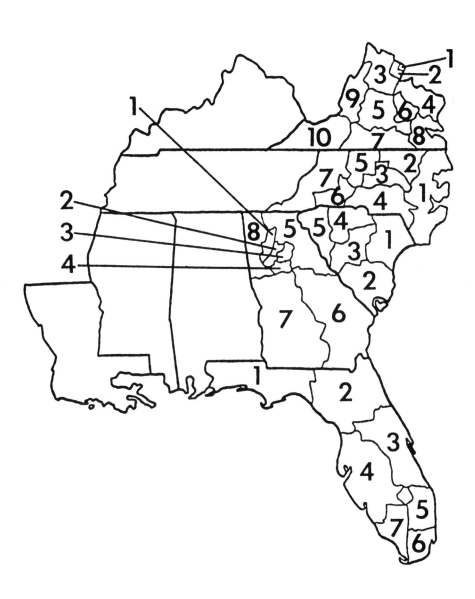

Southern Markets

Florida
1. Panhandle
2. Crown
3. East Central
4. West Central
5. Broward County, Martin County, and Palm Beach County
6. Dade County
7. Collier County, Hendry County, and Monroe County

Georgia
1. Cherokee County, Cobb County, and Douglas County
2. Fulton County
3. De Kalb County and Gwinnett County
4. Clayton County, Fayette County, Henry County, and Rockdale County
5. Northeast Georgia
6. Southeast Georgia
7. Southwest Georgia
8. Northwest Georgia

North Carolina
1. Coastal Plains
2. East Central
3. Research Triangle
4. Sand Hills
5. North Piedmont
6. South Piedmont
7. Western North Carolina

South Carolina
1. Pee Dee
2. Low Country
3. Mid Lands
4. East Piedmont
5. West Piedmont

Virginia
1. Arlington and Alexandria
2. Fairfax County
3. North Central Virginia
4. Northern Neck
5. Central Virginia
6. Richmond
7. Southside Virginia
8. Tidewater
9. Shenandoah
10. Southwest Virginia

Appendix C: Stability of Market Segment Distribution

The Market Segment Model shows how the geographic limits of students' collegiate aspirations are associated both with the socioeconomic characteristics of the markets in which those students live and with the availability of local higher education opportunities. Neither the socioeconomic character of a particular community nor the number of college and university spaces in that community is likely to change significantly in a short time period. For this reason, we expect that in a given market the distribution of students into market segments will remain reasonably stable from year to year. To test this assumption, we have analyzed three years of data for Pennsylvania students, studying the stability of market segment distributions in Pennsylvania over the period 1979 to 1981, with a brief look back at 1977.

In our pilot project, the first set of SAT-taking students classified were 1979 high school seniors from Pennsylvania. Included in this group were students who had taken the SAT in their junior year (1978), in their senior year (1979), or in both years. Pennsylvania was partitioned into thirteen markets: the five separate counties of the Philadelphia area, Allegheny County, and the seven remaining educational planning regions as defined by the Pennsylvania Department of Education. Since Pennsylvania originally was studied without reference to the other states in the Middle States region, we used only three market segments: local, in-state, and regional/national.

An examination of the data from 1980 and 1981 revealed considerable variance in the market segment distributions among markets but virtually no statistically significant change between years in segment distributions within the same market.[1] For example, the percentage of students classified as in-state in 1980 varied from a low of 9 percent in Philadelphia County to a high of 64.9 percent in Planning Region 7, while in 1981 the percentage of in-state students varied from a low of 8.9 percent in Philadelphia County to a high of 65.6 in Planning Region 7. In fact, Table C-1 demonstrates that the largest shift across any market from 1980 to 1981 was 3.1 percentage points in Planning Region 5, while the smallest shift was only 0.1-percent change in Philadelphia County and in Planning Region 6. Furthermore, the largest and smallest shifts appear to have occurred in and out of all three market segments; so, on the average, the percentage of students classified as in-state across all of Pennsylvania increased only from 29.6 percent to 30.6 percent, at the expense of very small decreases in the proportion of both local and regional/national students.

In the 1979 pilot study, special treatment was given to records in which the student submitted scores to Pennsylvania State University. This special action resulted in a classification system in 1979 that differs slightly from that of 1980 or 1981. Thus, the 1979 to 1980 and the 1979 to 1981 shifts in distributions of students are somewhat larger than those of 1980 to 1981. Nevertheless, a remarkable level of stability was exhibited even in these periods.

Data also were collected for the 1977 Pennsylvania testing cycle. Comparing the 1977 market segment distributions with those of any other year, we find substantial shifts over time in the proportion of students in a given segment of a single market. The 1977 data, however, differ from the data for subsequent years in that students who took the SAT in their junior year were excluded in 1977. When we compare data for 1977 and 1979, we find major decreases in the proportion of in-state students for every market. Junior-year-only test takers thus appear to behave differently from their senior-year test-taking classmates, since the former concentrate their choices either locally or nationally.

We conclude from these analyses that given a consistent set of classification criteria and a consistent set of criteria for inclusion of data in the study, we find little disturbance of the market segment distribution from year to year. Only after long periods, during which the economic and social characteristics of a region may change, do we expect to see significant swings in the market segment distribution.

Susan Shaman
Associate Director,
Higher Education Finance
Research Institute

Notes

1. Using the binomial test of proportions, we discovered that the only hypotheses barely rejected at the 0.01-percent level were no difference in the regional/national segment of Planning Region 5 and no difference in the in-state segment of Montgomery County.

Table C.1. Changes in Market Segment Distribution of Pennsylvania Students from 1980 to 1981

Market	Percent in 1980			Percent in 1981			Difference in 1980–81		
	Local	In-State	Regional/National	Local	In-State	Regional/National	Local	In-State	Regional/National
Bucks County	37.0	28.2	34.8	35.4	31.0	33.6	1.6	-2.8	1.2
Chester County	26.3	27.7	46.0	27.1	28.7	44.2	-0.8	-1.0	1.8
Delaware County	49.6	17.6	32.7	50.1	17.0	32.9	-0.5	0.6	-0.2
Montgomery County	35.4	22.0	42.5	34.8	25.0	40.1	0.6	-3.0	2.4
Philadelphia County	63.2	9.0	27.8	63.8	8.9	27.4	-0.6	0.1	0.4
Planning Region 2	20.3	50.4	29.3	20.9	50.4	28.7	-0.6	0.0	0.6
Planning Region 3	32.5	43.2	24.3	32.7	44.3	23.0	-0.2	-1.1	1.3
Planning Region 4	25.8	46.7	27.5	26.0	46.3	27.8	-0.2	0.4	-0.3
Planning Region 5	29.2	37.5	33.3	31.7	38.1	30.2	-2.5	-0.6	3.1
Planning Region 6	22.9	42.7	34.4	23.1	42.6	34.3	-0.2	0.1	0.1
Planning Region 7	11.1	64.9	24.0	12.9	65.6	21.5	-1.8	-0.7	2.5
Planning Region 8	45.5	16.9	37.6	45.1	17.3	37.6	0.4	-0.4	0.0
Allegheny County	49.0	21.6	29.4	47.5	23.3	29.2	1.5	-1.7	0.2
Total	37.8	29.6	32.6	37.6	30.6	31.8	0.2	-1.0	0.8

Appendix D: SAT-Score Submission and Matriculation: A Comparative Analysis

The Market Segment Model is primarily a vehicle for measuring institutional visibility as defined by patterns of SAT-score submission. Inevitably, however, questions are raised about the relationship between SAT-score submission and matriculation. Do students actually enroll in institutions located within the geographical boundaries described by their market segment classification? For instance, do high school seniors classified as local eventually enroll at colleges or universities located in the same market area as their home residences? The purpose of this appendix is to present the available evidence on where these SAT-taking students finally matriculate.

Data from the Pennsylvania Higher Education Assistance Agency (PHEAA) provided us with a unique opportunity to study this question. Table D-1 describes the results of merging CUEPP and PHEAA data for 1979 and 1981. In 1979, a total of 50,784 Pennsylvania high school seniors applied to PHEAA for financial assistance. Of these students, 43,413 were matched with individuals in the CUEPP file, yielding a merge rate of 85.5 percent. In 1981, the rate improved slightly to 89.9 percent.

While a substantial number of individuals are represented in these two merged files, it is important to note what the characteristics were of the unmerged CUEPP records. Table D-2 compares the merged test takers with the total high school test takers in 1979 and 1981. Among the classified test takers, slightly over half of the total test takers were merged, with the exception of those students classified as regional/national in 1979. However, there is a systematic bias among the unmerged CUEPP records. Because the PHEAA records are limited to those students seeking financial aid, one would expect that those high school seniors not applying for aid would come from more affluent families. This situation, in fact, turns out to be the case. In 1979, for instance, 41 percent of the unmerged CUEPP records had student-reported family incomes in excess of $20,000. If one assumes that the bulk of those students not reporting their family income come from more-affluent families and therefore were not applying for a PHEAA grant, then up to two-thirds of the 1979 CUEPP records involve students with substantial family incomes.

After merging the records in the CUEPP and PHEAA files, we linked the College Board and PHEAA college identification codes in order to determine where

Table D.1. Results of Merging PHEAA to CUEPP Files

	1979	1981
High School Seniors Applying for PHEAA Grants/Guaranteed Student Loans	50,784	56,077
Merged Records	43,413	50,406
Merge Rate	85.5	89.9

Table D.2. Results of Merging CUEPP to PHEAA, by Market Segment

	1979			1981		
	Local	*In-State*	*Regional/ National*	*Local*	*In-State*	*Regional/ National*
Classified Test Takers	29,936	23,286	23,366	27,295	22,180	23,120
Merged Test Takers	15,410	12,798	10,120	16,468	14,100	12,987
Merge Rate	51.5	55.0	43.3	60.3	63.6	56.2

the student eventually matriculated. In developing this linkage, two major categories of exceptions were identified: those merged students without a valid PHEAA code and those merged students for whom there was no corresponding college code in the College Board institutional listing. Merged students without a PHEAA college code could include students who matriculated at postsecondary education institutions considered to be ineligible by PHEAA or students who did not matriculate at all. If the latter case applies, these individuals provide an interesting study group of potential college students who carry with them a noncollege option that they eventually activate. The number of students in this category increased between 1979 and 1981. Merged students without a PHEAA–CUEPP link are students matriculating at postsecondary education institutions (typically proprietary schools) without College Board identifiers. While resource constraints limited our ability to locate these institutions relative to the student's home residence, there is no reason to believe that enrollment patterns would contradict market segment classification for these students.

**Table D.3. Percentage of Classified Students Who Matriculated
in the Identified Market Segment**

	Local	*In-State*	*Regional/ National*
1979			
Students with a valid PHEAA–CUEPP institutional ID	10,619	8,280	5,237
Percentage matriculating in the identified market segment	75	70	39
1981			
Students with a valid PHEAA–CUEPP institutional ID	10,095	8,186	5,615
Percentage matriculating in the identified market segment	79	72	34

Table D.3 presents our answer to the basic question raised in this appendix. Focusing on those merged students with a valid PHEAA–CUEPP institutional link, we can estimate the percentage of students who matriculated at colleges or universities located within the geographic boundaries described by their market segment classifications. A review of the data in this table yields three conclusions:

- At least three-fourths of the high school seniors classified as local eventually matriculate at an institution that is located in the same market area as their home residence.
- At least 70 percent of the high school seniors classified as in-state eventually matriculate at an institution located beyond the market of their home residence but still within the Commonwealth of Pennsylvania.
- Slightly more than a third of the students classified as regional/national eventually matriculate beyond Pennsylvania's borders.

The Market Segment Model appears to be least accurate in predicting the location of the regional/national students' eventual institution of matriculation. Several interpretations are possible. First, while these students consider out-of-state institutional options, they are very likely to develop several institutional options within Pennsylvania and perhaps close to home. Thus, we could expect increased variability among regional/national students due to the sheer number of in-state institutional options they develop. Second, recall that these students are applying for financial assistance and are, therefore, somewhat constrained by limited family resources. The unsubstantiated implication is that high school seniors from more-affluent families would not be as constrained. As we have seen, the character of unmerged CUEPP records tends to support such a theory. A third interpretation is that a student's home state exerts an attractive force in the student's college choice decision. It may be that the psychological barriers represented by state boundaries are stronger than the financial barriers involved in the college choice process.

The special case of regional/national data in this instance does not contradict our general validation of the model. Overall, the available evidence suggests that when a high school senior describes via SAT score submissions how far from home she or he is willing to travel to attend college, that senior is likely to matriculate at an institution within the specified geographical boundaries.

Michael Tierney
*Associate Director,
Higher Education Finance
Research Institute*

Selected Bibliography

Like all researchers, we have benefited from the work and insights of others. While enrollment research has proved a limited vineyard, a number of important studies and essays deserve particular recognition and acknowledgment.

Ahlberg, Dennis, Crimmuns, Eileen M., and Easterlin, Richard A. "The Outlook for Higher Education: A Cohort Size Model of College-Age Population, 1948–2000." *Review of Public Data Use* (1981) 9:211–27.

Bowen, Howard. *The Costs of Higher Education.* San Francisco: Jossey-Bass, 1980.

Cartter, Allan M. *Ph.D's and the Academic Labor Market.* New York: McGraw-Hill, 1976.

Centra, J. A. *College Enrollments in the 1980s: Projections and Possibilities.* New York: The College Board, 1978.

Doerman, Humphrey. *Toward Equal Access.* New York: The College Board, 1978.

Dresch, Stephen. "Demography, Technology, and Higher Education: Towards a Formal Model of Education Adaptation." *Journal of Political Economy* (1975) 85:535–69.

Easterlin, Richard A. *Birth and Fortune: The Impact of Numbers on Personal Welfare.* New York: Basic Books, 1980.

Freeman, Richard B. *The Overeducated American.* New York: Academic Press, 1976.

Ihlanfeldt, William. *Achieving Optimal Enrollments and Tuition Revenues.* San Francisco: Jossey-Bass, 1980.

Litten, Larry H., Sullivan, Daniel, and Brodigan, David. *Applying Market Research in College Admissions.* New York: The College Board, 1983.

Radner, Roy, and Miller, Leonard S. *Demand and Supply in U.S. Higher Education.* New York: McGraw-Hill, 1975.

Solomon, Lewis, and Taubman, Paul, eds. *Does College Matter?* New York: Academic Press, 1973.

Sewell, W. H., and Hauser, R. M. *Education, Occupation, and Earnings.* New York: Academic Press, 1975.

Wachter, Michael. "Economic Challenges Posed by Demographic Changes." In Eli Ginsberg et al., *Work Decisions in the 1980s.* Boston: Auburn House, 1982.